THE
BODY
LANGUAGE
OF
POLITICS

D0036995

PRAISE FOR *THE BODY LANGUAGE OF POLITICS*

"An excellent analysis of an important issue. Body language is important to understand because it does not lie, and politicians sometimes do! Fascinating exploration of the unfair comparisons between men and women political figures too. A must-read for candidates and active citizens."

　　　　—Gerald D. McCormick II, former House Majority Leader,
Tennessee General Assembly

"This book is direct, provocative, and timely given the political events thrown at us now hourly. It's a must read as 2020 approaches with fury. Body language tells us a lot especially when our choices are the 'evil of two lessers.'"

　　　　—Zach Wamp, member of US Congress 1995–2011

"Year after year, Gallup conducts a public poll that consistently highlights members of Congress as the least honest professionals in our society. Wouldn't it be great to have an instruction manual that helps us separate reality from fabrication in the communication habits of our political leaders? Fortunately, we now have such a resource. Dr. Van Natten's latest book is a must-have, particularly in our current political climate."

　　　　—Curt Lox, PhD, Dean of Brooks College of Health,
University of North Florida

"In the era of fake news and lying politicians, who can you trust? It may just come down to what they don't say—their body language. In *The Body Language of Politics*, Dr. Donna Van Natten challenges our own emotional bias toward certain politicians by exposing the deceptions found in their non-verbal communication. This is a true eye-opener and a game changer to inform our voting decisions."

　　　　—Marcel Schwantes, podcaster,
founder of Leadership from the Core

"My highest praise for this incredibly insightful and inspirational book. Dr. Donna Van Natten's insight and guidance on the importance and awareness of understanding our individual levels of bias, prejudice, and emotional intelligence, is an absolute "winner" and a must read for leaders and managers at all levels. *The Body Language of Politics* is a great way to "check" our own beliefs and behaviors and a gift for those seeking excellence and truth in our politicians at all levels! Thank you for a great and impactful read!"

—Maj. Robert Darling, President & CEO of Quantitative Analytics, LLC, author of *24 Hours Inside the President's Bunker: 9-11-01: The White House*

"This is a fascinating insight into the subliminal messages we send though our everyday actions. Dr. Van Natten carefully guides the reader through the verbal, non-verbal, and sociological aspects of human interaction and how impactful and consequential they can be. Any leader, whether political or organizational, will benefit from reading this book."

—Jim M. Coppinger, Hamilton County Mayor, Tennessee

THE BODY LANGUAGE OF POLITICS

DECIDE WHO IS LYING, WHO IS SINCERE, AND HOW YOU'LL VOTE

DR. DONNA VAN NATTEN

FOREWORD BY JOE NAVARRO

Skyhorse Publishing

Skyhorse Publishing books may be purchased in bulk at special discounts for sales promotion, corporate gifts, fund-raising, or educational purposes. Special editions can also be created to specifications. For details, contact the Special Sales Department, Skyhorse Publishing, 307 West 36th Street, 11th Floor, New York, NY 10018 or info@skyhorsepublishing.com.

Skyhorse® and Skyhorse Publishing® are registered trademarks of Skyhorse Publishing, Inc.®, a Delaware corporation.

Visit our website at www.skyhorsepublishing.com.

10 9 8 7 6 5 4 3 2 1

Library of Congress Cataloging-in-Publication Data is available on file.

Cover design by Tom Lau
Cover photo credits: Getty Images

Print ISBN: 978-1-5107-5120-0
Ebook ISBN: 978-1-5107-5122-4

Printed in the United States of America

To Evan, Jarrett, and Jillian
No memory is worth remembering without you in it.

Contents

Foreword

Not a week goes by where I am not scouring here and there for something worthwhile to broaden my understanding of nonverbal communications. Whether it's for business, for relationship building, or best practices, my mind is keen to learn from others and gain new insights.

Since 1971, I have pursued, with ever greater appreciation, the myriad of catalysts that influence our behaviors and make us uniquely communicative, diverse, and, thus, human. We are so different than all other mammals—we are the only species that can suspend disbelief and allow ourselves to be tricked into believing the fictional. When we cry in sympathy for a beloved character in a play, we are in a way displaying how vulnerable we are to something that is entirely fictional. In the same way we are moved by symbols, be it a flag that stirs our patriotism or a banner that affirms our unity with a winning team. We think we are very rational in everything we do, when in fact, we should take pause, which is why I am always looking to learn what else should I know about the things that cause our behavior or influence our decisions.

Finding books that add to the current state of knowledge, that make us think and ponder, are not that common. How often does a book come around that makes you not just think, but also makes you observe the world differently and makes you question how you see the world? That same eagerness for greater knowledge is shared by many, not just me.

And so, imagine my joy when I received *The Body Language of Politics* by Dr. Donna Van Natten in my mailbox. I am so very pleased she wrote this book. It fulfills my yearning to know: *What more is there? What have I missed? What should I be looking for or examining? What have others observed that I have missed? Have I considered this?* The book accomplishes all of that succinctly and with the kind of ample research one should expect from a seasoned expert. So with delight I devoured the book with an impish glee that I was being granted access to this material before the general public and I would have the benefit of this knowledge in advance of others.

With this work, Dr. Van Natten tackles a very interesting subject that is both consequential and timely—that is, how do nonverbal communications influence politics? I am not sure twenty-five years ago this topic could have been addressed as authoritatively as it is here because we now know so much more about what influences humans. The decisions we make every day that we think are so rational and so cognitively based, are in fact made on shaky ground. As Dr. Van Natten quickly shows us from the ample research, we humans are often seduced by such seemingly trivial things as: height, weight, gender, color of skin, even the superficial beauty of a candidate. Seemingly unimportant, and yet we attach so much importance to them; after all, isn't that often how we chose our mates?

Why this deep dive into how we are influenced matters is because character drives behavior, temperament drives behavior, worthiness drives the behavior of those we elect, and yet we often elect individuals not on these consequential traits, but rather, on superficial traits that are nothing more than cosmetic at best or manipulative and deceitful at worst.

Even if you are up on the literature of social engineering and nonverbal communications you will be pleasantly surprised at how Dr. Van Natten brings this all together as a complete package for us to consider. This book is not just for the nonverbal aficionado, Dr. Van Natten has gone further than merely writing about nonverbals—she has performed a civic duty to prepare us for those important decisions we make when we elect officials.

I say civic duty because it is rare to find an author that enlightens us to the point where it compels us to look further, to do our due diligence, our civic responsibility—not tribal cheerleading or mindless, politically yoked subservience that seems so pervasive.

Whether we are considering the effect of gender on our decision making, to subconscious stereotyping, to the halo effect that some people seem to have, or the effect that the media has on us, these are all well examined for our consideration. As are our emotional biases, which may be psychologically comforting because they are familiar, but they infringe upon our ability to see objectively and with clarity.

Dr. Van Natten explores how informed decisions are being challenged, if not threatened, in unprecedented ways, which brings into question our own ability to justify how we make decisions. For those seeking answers, it is all here; one merely has to look at two things: the table of contents (amply focused) and the bibliography.

Perhaps most intriguing are the insights into our ability to detect when politicians are lying to us. When they are being deceptive, manipulative, or conniving, how can we know with any kind of assurance? What are the pitfalls of trying to establish veracity as we work our way through what at times seems a constellation of candidates? Dr. Van Natten's work is most helpful here, as this is our personal responsibility—not for the media to tell us who is honest and certainly not for talking heads, but rather, through our own efforts.

As I reflect back on this book, I am also mindful of what my job is, as a student of nonverbals, as an author, and in writing this foreword. My job is neither to summarize this work nor to act as a cheerleader. I leave that to others. My job is to ensure that you understand that this is not a trivial work, that it matters greatly, that it is timely, and that if it is an easy and engaging read, so much the better. If I merely said that you should read this book because you will be better for it and because our nation will be better for it and that is reason enough, then too I would have done my job. Period.

—Joe Navarro, former FBI Special Agent, lecturer, and author of the international bestseller, *What Every BODY is Saying*

CHAPTER 1

The Political Landscape: An Analysis of the Media and Appearance

In the 1980s, experts began to see the significance of body language in politics. "[B]ody language may be the new communications signal in campaigns" (Griffith, 1984).

May be? I assure you that body language is the communication signal that steers our thoughts, emotions, judgments, and reactions. While we like to believe that our language and our bodies are two distinct, controllable entities, they are not. They constantly work in tandem to deliver messages to others.

Politicians must respect that communication is of great importance. Mastery of communication is key for success. Nonverbal communication provides an avenue to demonstrate this, and it must be intentional. Our body language, a significant part of nonverbal communication, demonstrates feelings, thoughts, and ideas for the masses.

Politics is the art of managing one's self. It is the business of impacting government while navigating complex relationships. It requires a savvy person who can meet the demands of individuals while simultaneously adhering to society's expectations.

More importantly, politics is image management. It must be closely monitored and controlled at all times. Both professionally and personally, a person in the twenty-four-hour spotlight must be keenly aware of the image he or she wants to present. One's nonverbals—defined as movements of one's body, gestures, expressions and sounds without using words, the use of time and space, and interactions with others—impact a leader's image. While most elements of this intricate formula are within a person's control, there remain situations in which the leader, the politician or candidate, has little or no control.

Every person, including politicians, leaves an imprint on others via management of ourselves or, lack thereof. As Sabuncuoglu (2005) suggests, "[i]mpressing others is placed in the basis of leadership." As humans, we learn from an early age that impressing other people gives us status and makes us stand out. So, mastering one's self is quite an art.

Nonverbals also strongly impact our view of how we communicate and influence others. As political candidates vie for top positions, there remains a specific personal profile for such leaders. Rooted in the literature, this impressive laundry list includes:

√   **Dominance**
√   **Empathy**
√   **Independence**
√   **Self-efficacy**
√   **Self-monitoring**

Add body language to that list. The challenge to display a strong, but empathetic, independent leader with self-control is daunting while ensuring that these traits come through one's nonverbals.

Look at the photographs below of leaders. Which traits would you assign to each politician? Do any display the traits that you personally expect from a leader? I predict you have a favorite and one you can't stand.

General Colin Powell.

Speaker Nancy Pelosi.

President George H. W. Bush.

We have high expectations for leaders—or at least we should. In addition to being leadership influencers, we also expect these persons to have charismatic personalities while possessing inspiration and motivation. If you think about it, it's a nearly impossible expectation.

We also believe that good leaders should maintain reserved body movements, demonstrate interest in the matter at hand, speak well, and interact with their followers. Deviate from these hidden rules, and suspicions quickly arise. These nonverbal rules are powerful; actually, they are more powerful than spoken words as confirmed by decades of communication research.

US Vice President Joe Biden and Republican vice presidential candidate US Rep. Paul Ryan participate in the vice presidential debate as moderator Martha Raddatz looks on at Centre College October 11, 2012 in Danville, Kentucky.

Remember the October 2012 debate between vice presidential candidates Republican Paul Ryan and Democrat Joe Biden? At times throughout the debate, the candidates' dramatic facial expressions and verbal attacks captivated viewers. It was impossible to ignore the shifts in tone highlighting sarcastic, aggressive, slashing, and unhinged behaviors. There were several childish and rude nonverbals from both candidates—which did not go unnoticed by viewers. From vivid hand gestures, to laughing "at" the other candidate's response while tilting back in the chair, each candidate's body language reinforced his verbal message.

Leaders influence others by intentionally using their nonverbals, including eye contact, mannerisms, body movements, use of space, tone of voice, hand gestures, touch, smiling, and even walking with a "bounce in the step."

For example, the Prime Minister of the United Kingdom (1994-2007), Tony Blair, showed his anxiousness when he fiddled with his fingers. This subtle nonverbal, also known as "a tell," indicated a small gesture of self-soothing. While many may not have noticed, the savvy viewer always noticed. In the United States, President George W. Bush would bite the inside of his cheek when he was anxious. President Bill Clinton would intentionally bite his lower lip trying to appear emotional. There are hundreds of gestures and facial nonverbals that "tell" one's inner thoughts, hold our attention, and speak to us—though not necessarily through the mouth.

British Prime Minister David Cameron and his wife Samantha Cameron (L) welcome former Prime Minister Gordon Brown and his wife, Sarah Brown to Number 10 Downing Street on July 24, 2012.

By making eye contact, the receiver instantly feels special—like he or she might be the only one in the room. Eyes also solicit emotional responses based on crying, movement of the muscles around the eyes, and condition of the health of the eyes. Strong and sustained eye contact while speaking with someone draws us in. "Look into my eyes." We might even call it rather captivating.

Kamala Harris as she visits the outside of a detention center for migrant children.

Most of us were raised to be on our best behaviors when in public. We were raised to use good manners. This basic expectation is also expected of politicians, so when we watch a leader with bad manners, uncertainties arise. Regardless of role or title, gracious hosts are more attractive and appealing. Bad manners are just that—bad.

We quickly react when we see someone, especially an adult, have a temper tantrum. We'll even stare at this person as he or she becomes unhinged. While we may be amused, we do not like it. We especially do not like it from our leaders. As we watch these unbecoming nonverbal body behaviors in action, we also take into consideration the person's proximity to us to and the ill-behaved person's physicality in specific spaces. All these are important clues for reading body language.

Command of one's physical space, including stage, room, and office influences our perceptions of leaders. One's use of proxemics, or the amount of space one feels necessary between self and others, is a critical aspect of body language. During the town hall debate on October 9, 2016 at Washington University, two candidates' actions and words left their mark on us, the viewers and voters. Then-candidate Donald Trump often made the most of the debate stage when Hilary Clinton would speak. Some argue that he violated her space by coming too close or even looming behind her. Others say he commanded the stage.

Democratic presidential nominee former Secretary of State Hillary Clinton (R) speaks as Republican presidential nominee Donald Trump listens during the town hall debate at Washington University on October 9, 2016 in St Louis, Missouri.

The media, of course, rushed in to discuss Trump's negative and overbearing body language during this heavily televised debate. A quick Google search (July 2019) on the topic yielded more than 2.8 million results. According to Clinton's memoir *What Happened*, "Trump made [her] feel incredibly uncomfortable and was breathing down [her] neck, while pacing behind [her]." Further, Clinton shared, "Do you stay calm, keep smiling, and carry on as if he weren't repeatedly invading your space? Or do you turn, look him in the eye and say loudly and clearly: 'Back up you creep, get away from me. I know you love to intimidate women, but you can't intimidate me, so back up.'" There's a strong chance that Trump was intentional with this course of action.

On the other end of the scale, use of space can leave us with a feeling of satisfaction and preference for a candidate. President Obama was known for walking stately across stages, drifting back and forth to capture and engage with his audiences. This broad physical nonverbal action connected the president with people.

Yet, there are those of us who may not connect or identify with a particular person or are on the fence. In cases like these, scholars share that the needs of these "leaderless groups" include a host of expectations, including:

- √ Verbal expressiveness
- √ Effectiveness
- √ Individual prominence
- √ Group goal facilitation
- √ Group sociability
- √ Physical energy
- √ Intelligence
- √ Emotional stability

We may not have even thought about the significance of each of these requirements, but they are important on a subconscious level. Those in search of a leader look at the physical and emotional stability of a candidate. People seek out a leader who values group dynamics and needs by requiring leaders to have strong verbal and social skills.

As we look for leaders who possess specific traits, we should not overlook the type of leadership we want, and which one draws us in.

Leadership styles fall into three broad categories with prescriptive subsets. Transformational leadership, transactional leadership, and laissez-faire leadership are specifically discussed because leaders select one type to drive their message and keep followers.

Transformational leadership requires the leader to be optimistic, excited, and future-driven. This leader must be able to influence others while communicating values, purpose, and mission. Through intellectual stimulation, a transformational leader attacks problems with solutions. Simultaneously, the transformational leader develops, mentors, and attends to individual needs of his or her followers. Prescribed behaviors of this style require going above and beyond with a strong vision. As you read this, you might even be thinking that this style of leadership is rather optimistic, but hard to deliver. From a nonverbal perspective, we might see a candidate leaning in to listen to a voter's question, or excessively smiling while shaking hands to indicate warmth and authenticity. Strong eye contact, or gazing, is used to let receivers know that they are important.

Transactional leadership, on the other hand, entails a relationship between reward and punishment between the leader and followers. Rewards are distributed when followers perform well. This leader uses a passive approach to keep score of mistakes and failures. He or she may wait to intervene based on the severity of the issue. Active and passive are words often used to describe this type of leadership style. This style tends to be associated with the masculine, as well. Do you know someone like this? Nonverbals may include scowling, scolding, and aggressive facial expressions with a lot of grand hand gestures like finger pointing and raised fists followed by booming word choices. We might even see the bottom teeth similar to how a dog growls when threatened.

The third style which some leaders opt for is **laissez-faire leadership**, which is a failure to actively engage during critical times. With this type of leadership, little responsibility is noted from the leader along with little or no regard for followers. With minimal or no interference, this leader just goes with whatever dice have been rolled. For some, this is a frustrating style in that no transformation and action are seen. Body language in this type may include little to zero facial expressions, reserved body gestures, or remaining still and poised. Little rattles this type of leader.

Given these specific leadership styles, both transformational and transactional leadership styles are considered effective political styles. We tend to align ourselves with one of these two in order to have a say or participatory role in politics or government. Which one do you prefer? Recent presidents have displayed nonverbals respective of each style.

We also assign status to people who can bring something to us. They may have something that we desire, so by aligning with them, we elevate them to a status that helps advance our personal and political agendas.

Leaders are actors, too. Think about performers turned politicians and their mastery of looking like leaders. From actor turned president, Ronald Reagan, to entertainer turned congressman, Sonny Bono, these actor-leaders have perfected the role of what we believe we want in a leader. In actuality, dozens of actors (and just a few actresses) have transitioned from leading man to leader. In addition to Reagan and Bono, the list includes Arnold Schwarzenegger, Clint Eastwood, Al Franken, Jesse Ventura, Fred Thompson, and Jerry Springer to name a few. Oh, and Cynthia Nixon, too. These people had celebrity status prior to entering politics, thereby they made the transition easier with name recognition.

It shouldn't go unnoticed that all but one of the actors and entertainers I mentioned are middle-aged white males. Add President Donald Trump to that. His fame as a TV personality and popular TV show host of *The Apprentice* helped elevate his status among the general public. And, who can forget his famous slogan of "You're fired." Talk about a communication tactic that worked!

A sustainable leader must do a lot. They must know their audience, use persuasion, ignore protests, act like the audience is a part of the production, respect the audience's feelings, imbed trust and respect during speeches, avoid rambling, and use body language to support the verbal message. These are heavy-duty requirements for speaking and challenge even the best orators. Yet, leaders with status get passes because they are a part of our "in-group" and we see them more favorably.

This type of high status is usually freely granted to people who can benefit a group. Applied to positions with a lot of power, like the office of the president, individuals are elevated because they promise to meet the needs of the group and share similar ideologies. In other high-status offices, a person is elevated under these similar conditions. Once admiration is earned, or unearned, the rise to the top is important for understanding how we perceive our favored leaders. This may help us understand how President Trump, with very limited political experience, secured America's top government position. He first entertained us every week on TV.

Humans are visual creatures; it's our primary sense for processing information. Today's sharing of information is visual. So, it would make sense that the media would capitalize on this by its use of images and videos. By splashing photos everywhere, we are able to quickly look at an image and draw a conclusion, or at least, focus on the image to gather more information about it. Have you noticed that TV anchors politely warn us about the "disturbing images we are about to see" and proceed to blow up our screens with them?

Lest we forget, the paparazzi often trample over each other to nab the perfect photo and then unabashedly sell it to the highest bidder. Images are that powerful. And, in low information situations, our assessment of nonverbals is heightened as we judge the image and watch the video. When we don't know something or haven't done the research, we default to what we see to provide information and judgment. The almighty media giants know this, too.

Media outlets are intimately intertwined with our personal and professional decisions, including voting preferences. We have twenty-four-hour news access and most media sources unapologetically sway us to support one party or person. Depending on how interviews are edited for maximum viewing with blatant interviewer bias, we are influenced, swayed, and committed to what we see. Forget the truth—just subscribe to your favorite channel or celebrity. Media helps the average person "make sense" of complex political and social issues in our country by validating or producing reasonable rationales. We just accept this for the most part.

Politicians also engage with the media to mold how they develop their image, share information, and make assertions based on their current roles or positions. But I urge you to remember that bias in the media is real. If time is money, then screen time is currency for the mega-rich.

Further, no news is bad news. When candidates receive a lot of airtime, we take notice. Photos influence us. Front page photos above the fold of the newspaper are ideal for recognition. Few of us turn the newspaper pages or scroll down online stories to read the details. It's just not that important.

Visual politics is considered an important field in that most Americans receive their "education" and information from this source. "Perception politics" is yet another term used as we think about our perceptions of candidates based on extreme visual imagery. While we used to get most of our information from tabloids, TV, and newspapers, today's clickbait-driven world with instant responses has brought the role of visual politics into a whole new realm. With this, as we know, comes biased, slanted, fake news, and inference interwoven with facts and data. I wonder, how do we know what to believe?

Framing candidates' nonverbals is important towards forming our opinions of them, as is airtime, journalist bias, and how candidates persuade us. Much of this is done through candidates' faces glowing from our television screens. This was clearly documented during one 2000 Gore and Bush debate study in which viewers watched the candidates' nonverbals to determine who looked more "hopeful, intelligent, and caring" versus who looked "out of touch and afraid." Viewer perception assigned the positive characteristics to Al Gore and thought George Bush had significantly more negative nonverbal behaviors.

Yet, do we believe what we see or what we hear? Scholars repeatedly confirm that seeing is more powerful than just listening to the rhetoric we are used to hearing as part of the debate and campaign process. Bucy and Grabe's (2007) longitudinal study examined image and sound bites between the 1992 to 2004 presidential campaigns and concluded that total campaign coverage focused on images much more than sound bites. And, when sound bites were aired, they were "found to be largely attack and issue focused."

Armed with this knowledge, news programs spend a huge amount of time and money covering the candidates with carefully selected images and sound bites during election years. Contender highlights, clips, scandals, and other topics are aired and discussed for hours. The media is well aware of the significance of producing captivating visual images to hook and hold us, the viewers and voters. As a result of keeping us engaged, we remember what we see, how we feel, and, in the end, how we'll judge. Then, we take our feelings to the voting booths. May we always remember that "the future of this republic is in the hands of the American voter," as President Dwight D. Eisenhower proclaimed.

Nonverbal communication is an important process as it provides a wealth of information about someone's emotional state and intentions. This form of communication, if performed well, is a successful tool for politicians to garnish support and loyalty from followers.

With never-ending waves of social media crashing upon us, everyone now has the ability to ride a wave with their voices, opinions, and judgements. No longer are we dependent on being fed information from television networks, radio announcers, and big city newspapers. And, even though many traditional news outlets are thriving, they remain controlled by politically savvy owners who closely monitor viewer ratings.

Think back to when television came into our living room and men anchored the news. Much time was given to the story and it was rich with details. In today's world, there has been a big shift. The greater percent of airtime has shifted to diverse teams of news anchors, subject experts, and on-the-scene journalists. Subject experts now sit around the table to give their opinions while tabletop banter entertains us. Even online, a few quotes from politicians themselves spark journalist rants, often without much attention to the actual politician's statements in its full context. Today, clips are short (less than twenty seconds) and we move on to devour more with one simple swipe. Yet, research confirms that these "thin slices" of activity enable us, the viewer, to process and make decisions.

Network TV knows this and is considered a primary source of campaign information for most viewers. A wealth of research on how we see our candidates and leaders televised continues to stress that viewers rely heavily on visual images. Therefore, TV and social media videos and photographs are ideal for telling us what the candidates want us to know about them. Television remains an effective source for information and smart phones have made it common place to take our mini screens with us wherever we go—even to the bathroom. No longer must we rush home to see the evening news. At any time, twenty-hour hours a day, we have access to visual information.

During the 1980s Reagan-Bush campaigns, Bucy and Grabe (2007) found that campaign visuals were extensively used in news reports. This clever form of candidate advertising included a particular story structure, shorter air times, and faster delivery to capture viewers. By quickly engaging viewers, we were able to watch a slew of nonverbal activities within shorter time frames.

Additionally, the length of sound bites has declined over the decades while journalist talk time has increased. News professionals are now a part of the visual story. Often, three or four of them team up to interview and drill a candidate on the issues and, in the end, share their own views about the candidate.

The use of electronic media is increasing, and politicians are forced to use these methods of communication to get their message out. With a continual decrease in sound bites, we have shifted our attention to visual significance. Visual content consumes our screens. From the chiming and dinging of cell phones to the glow of eighty-inch flat screens, we are bathed in direct visual cues from candidates and incessant commentaries from political experts and news teams.

The popularity of split TV screens has enabled us to watch at least two candidates at a time interact and watch the back and forth question/answer process between journalist and candidate. Simultaneously, we are now able to watch and assess the immediate reactions to what someone says or does as a part of a debate—complete with bantering and long-winded interview questions. For example, during one 2012 Obama-Romney debate, viewers actually saw Obama wince when Romney attacked an issue. These real-time reactive behaviors gave us the chance to draw our own conclusions between candidates. This type of body language is key for us to make informed decisions.

TV also amplifies expressive displays and we draw conclusions from even the smallest of nonverbals glaring from our screens. Gong and Bucy (2016) found that "exposure to just a minute or two of tel-evised political exchange allows viewers to make fine-grained assess-ments of candidate performance, accurately identify who is more social dominant and articulate reasons why and infer a variety of trait characteristics based on observed candidate behavior." Wow— all that in one minute! It's no surprise that we are bombarded with campaign ads and commercials during election years. We know the power of a good commercial. Heck, the Superbowl banks on it! So do political campaigns.

And, do we trust more what we see or hear? When the two don't match, research constantly confirms that we default to what we see. "Viewers may concentrate on the visual aspect of the presentation and ignore the verbal message to reduce cognitive overload" (Gong and Bucy, 2016). While watching televised debates, I suggest you watch who is not speaking. Process their actions and reactions against the knowledge you have about them. Remember that their nonver-bals might be quick, but they provide us with powerful data.

Let's consider the first televised debate between Richard Nixon and John F. Kennedy in 1960. At that time, about eighty-five percent of American households had at least one television. This debate was a rare opportunity for viewers to see their candidate in action and watch their nonverbals. Many huddled around the TV to watch the debate between the two. As most know, Kennedy easily triumphed, and viewers formed positive impressions based on what they saw. Nixon suffered as a result of this aired debate. The primary reasons for this outcome were Kennedy's captivating nonverbals and Nixon's ancillary conditions.

Prior to the debate, Nixon had hurt his knee on a car door and it subsequently became infected. When he arrived at CBS studios, he hit it again, causing incredible pain and discomfort which many described as the color "draining from his face." Makeup was applied to cover Nixon's dark circles and facial scruff, but hot studio lighting caused Nixon to sweat. Even before the debate started, Nixon's body language was a problem.

On the other side, tan-skinned Kennedy arrived free of any physical pain. His attractive looks and dashing smile did not go unnoticed by many as he strolled in with an air of confidence.

The conditions were perfect for Nixon to fail and Kennedy to prevail even before the debate started. Now, think about this for today's stage of contenders. What might be going on that may impact how they appear and perform? What personal or professional issues are plaguing them that they try hard to suppress? I believe that we probably haven't given it much thought. And, should we? Most likely the networks will show us what they want us to see.

Television is powerful and unaccountable. We don't get a choice as to its contents but remain the receivers of what we see and hear. Today, around ninety-six percent of households have at least one TV and/or one cell phone, and eighty-one percent of Americans also own a smartphone (Pew Research Center, 2019). The vast majority of Americans are digitally connected. As experts have announced, visual devices have created "a near revolutionary change in the democratic process." Adding to this visual overload, we are also subject to never-ending post-debate commentaries, blogs, TV talk shows, and tweets. From the analysis of every word to the dissection of every nonverbal, candidates are broken into micro-sized morsels and offered to the general public, complete with large doses of unsolicited commentaries.

The Internet also has changed how we communicate, learn, feel, and share information. Politically speaking, is it a platform in which the concepts of power, history, demographics, values, emotions, and thought converge to tell a story about politician and voter. Just by engaging online, we become active members of politics. We now have an in-group and feel emotionally connected.

We get to align with the in-group's cognitive agenda. In turn, we have also identified the out-group, or opponent—the one we blame and attack. Social media provides the vehicle for this rapid movement of thought, feeling, and action. And, the body language of candidates, politicians, and leaders is imbedded throughout.

The Internet has enabled us to have universal access to almost everyone through various communication mediums. As a part of this, the online battleground for power can either bond or break us. We have our favorite TV stations, news anchors, podcasts, and online personalities. And, they also have their preferred political parties and candidates. Nonpartisan news may sound good in theory, but is nearly impossible in reality. Our brains are thirsty for more and rarely are they quenched.

We want to see candidates vie for their spot and come out victorious. We see this through journalists' rapid firing of questions. Our preferred news style is one of "harrying, rapid-fire cross examination, not hostile but not chummy either" (Griffith, 1984). While that was found to be the norm thirty years ago, today's question-pelting and rebuttals are rather hostile.

As we often hear, appearances matter. So do gender, age, race, religion, and size. Yet, there has not been a slew of in-depth investigation on the intersection of race, gender, stereotypes, and roles in the public sector. Diversity comes in all shapes and sizes; therefore, as responsible citizens, we must understand the role of race, ethnicity, sexual orientation, age, religion, and other types of diversity because they impact how we pick leaders and vote.

It is well documented that female political leaders are harshly scrutinized based on their appearance. For example, a dress worn by the Prime Minister of the United Kingdom, Theresa May, outlined her breasts and became a source of public opinion. Labor Leader Emily Thornberry was known for wearing "Battle Dress." Politician Harriet Harman was deemed "dowdy" for her clothing choices. Past presidential candidate Hillary Clinton's pantsuits were often a source of debate. First Lady Melania Trump's jacket choice sent the media into overdrive trying to figure out what this jacket back actually meant as she visited Texas detention centers in 2018.

Melania Trump climbs back into her motorcade after traveling to Texas to visit facilities that house and care for children taken from their parents at the US-Mexico border on June 21, 2018.

In regards to the fashion choices of female politicians, Dr. Rhonda Garelick of the Parsons School of Design in New York City wrote that, "It's crucial not to reduce women to their appearance, that is all too easily and all too frequently done and a huge, sexist mistake. But that does not mean that we can't acknowledge, appreciate and interpret fashion as part of their (nonverbal) communications."

Everitt et al. (2016) found that men, more than women, disapproved of "visual dominance" when watching women. Meaning, men didn't like watching dominant females. Overall, though, female viewers, but not male viewers, were more positive about female politicians as they watched them during a campaign race. However, when males exhibited masculine motions, they were preferred by both genders.

For women, being less animated was favored by voters. Summarizing the findings from this study, when the media focused on female candidates' more assertive, masculine, and bigger nonverbal displays, they were inadvertently "condemning female candidates to lower agentic (masculine) assessments and a less sympathetic voting public."

It appears that women must always have "just the right amount of …" as part of their vitae. As if how you dress determines how you can run a country. Or, does her finger pointing remind you of your mother scolding you?

The media will target the physical appearance of a candidate and capitalize on it. One prime example was the weight of former Governor of New Jersey Chris Christie's during the 2016 election. Political writers, and even late night talk show hosts, had a field day with his weight. References included, "a fat slob," "elephant in the room," "fat as a bible-belt leader," and "morbidly obese." These slams alone would provide enough "evidence" for many voters to question his fitness for office. Offensive weight references, or even talking about one's physical appearance, drive news stories and splash across daily headlines. Check out the magazine racks the next time you are standing in a line at the grocery store. Count the number of weight references on the covers. Look at the detail given to how celebrities look. Yes, appearances make the headlines. It's a big deal.

Then-republican Presidential candidate New Jersey Governor Chris Christie holds a town hall meeting on February 8, 2016 in Manchester, New Hampshire.

Mocking one's weight also appears to be socially acceptable. When media sources attack politicians' weight, they infer a lack of personal discipline and control, and then assign it to that person's ability to lead. Research on US presidential elections even suggested that taller people were assigned the leader role and considered dominant. Along the same vein, higher status individuals were also seen as taller. Perhaps even bigger than life. Yet, these perceptions or assignments of value are not fact-based or true. At times, we struggle with the truths of what we know versus what we see and feel. One such feeling is age bias.

While thirty-five years old is the legal minimum age to run
for president, some question if there should be a maximum age
that someone could run for the office. Meaning, age is a factor for
how we view a candidate's fitness for office. Currently, our oldest
president was Ronald Reagan, at seventy-three years, 274 days old
at the time of his second term win. Our county's youngest president was John F. Kennedy at forty-three years, 163 days old. Of
course, recent senior citizens include President Donald Trump
(seventy-three years), Senator Bernie Sanders (seventy-seven years)
and former Vice President Joe Biden (seventy-six years). Voters are
clearly aware that they look older than the average age (fifty-five
years) of American presidents in our history.

Results from an age study concluded that older individuals
did not do as well as their younger opponents. They received less
favorable ratings in terms of hiring and were considered less physically fit and cognitively sharp. Meaning, the older you are, the more
out of shape and dim you are—regardless of gender or political
party. This makes sense to the average voter because we do not want
our president to have health issues or die while in office. The job is
demanding. The twenty-four-hour stamina and requirements are
taxing for even the fittest and sharpest—and youngest. The job ages
you. And, this is a job with a lot of airtime, so it's important that
our commander in chief look the part.

A crucial part of leading requires winning and beating others
who also want the job. For this, we have a process of "competition and elimination" (a.k.a. debate). This is an important event
for individuals in a group and who are leaderless. These groups will
work to find a leader and naturally utilize the debate process for
leader selection and leader emergence. During face-to-face interactions, extraversion and emotional stability predict emerging leaders.
Extroverted individuals are most likely to emerge as leaders in leaderless groups. These groups also consider intelligence and, to a lesser
extent, social skills.

As a part of the competition and elimination process, activities
are repeated until a leader finally emerges to meet the group's needs.

Apply this to how President Trump competed, gained popularity, and eventually eliminated all of the other qualified and seasoned Republican candidates during the 2016 presidential election. Trump's mastery of nonverbals, his physical presence in the middle of the pack, and his strong tone of voice no doubt played a significant role in increasing his status.

Commentary-style news programming has become normal in today's media and profits have soared. Think about *Fox & Friends*. By mere title alone, they state that they are giving us the news AND they are our friends. But I highly doubt they are everyone's buddy. TV news host Bill O'Reilly even stated that he aims to "arouse anger" in his audience (Weeks, 2016). *The Rachel Maddow Show* is described as "daily news and opinion" television. So, by tuning in, we expect her opinion; and we get it. Ratings confirmed that her show is a "leading outlet for criticism on President Trump." Many viewers feel emotionally aligned and loyal to Maddow. Experts confirm that these opinion-first programs are more biased and emotional. You should not be shocked when watching them.

When we watch the negativity in partisan news, this increases our anger and triggers emotions. We become focused on opposing candidates and, in a way, are at war. We have a party and/or person on which to place blame, and this person becomes the target, source, or scapegoat of what is wrong. Partisan news is powerful. It has the ability to not only evoke anger and anxiety from us, but it is able to focus these negative emotions towards specific candidates.

There is a "losing look" that's been documented by numerous researchers through hundreds of studies. Signs of defeat are clearly detectable and include exhaustion, fearful or stained expressions, body limpness, sorrowful and tired eyes, and softer breathing with less voice when speaking. The look on Ohio Democrat Rich Cordray's face clearly tells us that he has been defeated in 2018. The lowered eyes. The pursed mouth. The slumped head. The hand extended for comfort. These nonverbals say it all.

When we look down, it triggers a negative reaction in us similar to how we feel when someone avoids making eye contact. Simple acts break down confidence and lessen a candidate's status of leader, regardless of experience and fitness for the job. We want to see emotions so we can fully assess how a candidate uses his or her words, tone, and body to communicate.

Our country is politically polarized. It appears that everyone has an opinion about the current status of American government and politics. Loyalty shows up in how we act, react, behave, and talk during these challenging political times. And, voters rarely look at their own behaviors as indicative of how they might vote, be influenced, and judge what they deem as important. Being a member of a group allows us to collectively favor someone who we see with positive qualities and punish others who we see as exhibiting negative traits. This is known as the "black sheep effect" (Diermeier and Li, 2019).

Research confirms that greater polarization has led to more divergence among people which leads to reinforcing of mass thoughts simply by being a part of a particular group. Consider President Trump's masses of followers who proudly wear their red "Make American Great Again" hats and support whatever he says, does, and tweets. These visual artifacts quickly identify one's in-group status. These in-group masses are not concerned with getting to the nitty-gritty of policies, foreign affairs, and the like, but feel empowered just by being a part of the in-group. We want to look alike. And, looking alike can lead to acting or reacting alike.

Emotions in politics are used to persuade us. Political campaigns are unique in that they operate on opposite extremes. Research suggests that negative, bad, or alarming information, perceived or real, captures and holds us the most. When we watch the news and a special report interrupts our regularly broadcast show, we sit up and feel slightly anxious about the bad news we are about see. On the radio, the bells and alarms that occasionally break into our music or podcast prepare us for the worst. Even Amber Alerts startle us and make us wince inside knowing that a child is in danger. Regardless, we watch—constantly.

We are highly sensitive to negative influencers. Weeks (2016) points out that "stronger party identification leads to more negative emotional and physiological responses to political news." Anger, partisanship, and information sharing found that men shared information more than women, that mainstream news was the mechanism for sharing, and that those with less information shared more often.

Politicians must consider their body language and emotions as a part of their branding and engagement with viewers for whom they wish to win over. Candidates who operate from a pessimistic point of view are more likely to struggle and fail based on how people tolerate negative personalities. When President Obama first campaigned, Americans wanted hope. He won because a great leader will utilize his or her emotional toolbox to influence an audience and gather their support.

Subliminal threats also jolt us. When candidates speak of nuclear war or being on the brink of war, Americans go on emotional high alert. When political commercials tell us all about what could go wrong and why the other candidate is a threat to our national security or welfare, we cease up. The seed has been planted. Sitting presidents often get reelected during these times. No one votes for the unknown presidential candidate—incumbents have always won. Even President Abraham Lincoln's slogan, "Don't change horses in midstream" told voters to stay the course, and they did.

We tie emotions to our values and attitudes. Both are steadfast and, often, unwavering. In turn, a feeding frenzy approach emerges. Anger, plus motivation, increases political interest and the need for news to validate and reaffirm. Emotions get people to react.

I urge you to observe the body language of every candidate and the status you assign to your favorite candidate. Why do you pick one over another? What are your biases on age, religion, gender, size, and race? You have them—we all do. Own your emotions while watching what the media feeds you. Actually understand how the Internet and media outlets guide you with the slightest nudge. You must be intentional in your assignments of value and whom you give a pass to, regardless of what they do. Watch spilt TV screens, look for nonverbals to match or challenge what is said, and investigate. Gather information before you make your choice.

"Emotion always has its roots in the unconscious and
manifests itself in the body."
—Irene Claremont de Castillejo

CHAPTER 2

Knowing the Different (and Unfair) Gender Expectations Imbedded in Us

Gender and nonverbals are interconnected in terms of how voters evaluate their political choices. When political figures speak, nonverbal cues serve as triggers for how we react and view these higher status individuals. As a part of this, society has assigned gender specific nonverbals (act like a boy or act like a girl) to each sex, and these gender-based stereotypes or norms are at play when we engage with others.

Gender differences exist. As humans, how do we measure masculinity and femininity? While we usually can tell the difference between a male and a female, the degrees to which we assign masculinity and femininity are not as transparent. At play are biological and social factors, developmental influences, social expectations, and expected roles for each sex.

When we apply these gender-based rules and expectations to men and women, female leaders are, overall, perceived more negatively than male leaders, particularly when we need leader guidance or direction. It becomes a question of whom will we naturally follow?

In society, we have the expectation that men be assertive, strive for achievement, and be naturally competitive. For women, gender expectations include being a nurturer, acting benevolent, and caring for others. Women are expected to have communal characteristics and consider others' needs as a part of leadership; yet, this is not the case for men. One study found that fifty-nine percent of leadership emergence was based solely on traits to determine if a leader would be successful. As we can imagine, women are frequently under the microscope.

When gender-based factors are applied to leadership and how a president should lead our country, actions, promises, and expectations greatly vary. We have different expectations simply based on the gender we see. Societal norms dictate that women display communal behavers like sensitivity, service, and meekness—whereas, men are rewarded for ambition, dominance, assertiveness, control, and confidence. It is important to examine leadership situations as part of how we judge men and women in their roles as candidates, emerging leaders, or current higher status politicians.

When examining transformational leadership, which is both collaborative and power sharing, one would think that women leaders would have the advantage in terms of working with others and sharing via interpersonal relationships. Transactional leadership, as previously discussed, fails to consider these factors; for example, the current President Trump asserts his power and agendas on the masses with little consideration of follower impacts.

Specific to leadership styles, one interesting study found that women exceeded men in "overall" transformational leadership, especially on the individualized consideration subset which pertained to mentoring and people support. Men, on the other hand, fared better than women in management with "active and passive behaviors" and via laisse-faire leadership.

Transformational leadership is more congruent with the feminine and transactional with the masculine. The transformational leadership style encourages agreeableness and nurturing of others which are aligned with femininity. Some call these communal or agentic behaviors.

The style of leadership that they exude may be important for men, but not for women. For example, being inspiring is seen as necessary for the promotion of men; ergo, a sage male would include this style in his bid for promotion and electoral races. For women, both inspirational motivation and individualized consideration are deemed equally important characteristics for leadership advancement. Note, a double standard.

The "backlash effect" comes into play when each gender breaks from gender expectations. This is true for both women and men. For those who display counter-gender stereotypes, they may be penalized. However, when it comes to actions like decisiveness and boldness, women may actually be socially rewarded for stepping up and making hard choices.

When looking at the debate process, studies found that women did better when they remained calm and contained themselves. For example, when male candidates used assertive (often seen as aggressive) nonverbals, they received support from viewers. On the other hand, women were penalized for the same use of body language.

During the 2016 US presidential election, this composite image (below) taken from two different events makes us feel something about each presidential hopeful. Nonverbally, we see open mouths, tilted heads, strong eye contact, raised hands, suits, and half bodies above the podium—all factors which impact how we feel about these political candidates without knowing what is actually being said or argued. Take notice, though, how Clinton's photo is a close-up, making her nonverbals appear more aggressive when compared to Trump's mouthy display and hand gestures. A larger microphone may also suggest that Clinton's tone or volume is elevated, which many would find offensive. Her physical height literally puts her mouth closer to the microphone.

Another fascinating way to look at gender involves the type of task and how the task is framed. When certain tasks are framed as either masculine or feminine, perceptions change. Research confirms that female leaders are perceived more negatively than male leaders when "providing guidance or direction."

When a situation is labeled or looks communal, many think that women would be better suited to leadership than their male counterparts. This holds some truth based on the gender composition of the group. For example, when a group was primarily male, a woman "stood out" solely based on her gender. However, this was not necessarily the case for groups mainly comprised of women. The male did not receive the same degree of noticeability.

These gender stereotypes in leadership put aspiring women at a disadvantage solely based on their gender and prescribed expectations. If a woman acts feminine in a leadership role, she puts herself at great risk of being questioned for the role. If she "acts like a man" by displaying agentic or stereotypically masculine behaviors, she risks being labeled as inauthentic. Derogatory labels for crossing gender expectations can be harsh. I know you've heard them—have you used them, too?

Marine Corps recruit Kylieanne Fortin, of Williamsport, Maryland, goes through close combat training at the United States Marine Corps recruit depot.

When we are fearful and seek leadership, women leaders, overall, struggle to reach high ranking positions and be seen as effective compared to men.

In mixed gender company, such as debates or meetings, a female leader is still expected to default to her gender-expected behaviors, which may include being nice, considering the feelings of others, and nurturing the needs of the group. Needless to say, it is a challenging situation for a female in most leadership positions—particularly for the highest offices in America.

Studies found that when performance evaluations were conducted on both women and men in leadership positions, women received lower ratings for similar tasks. They also were not promoted to higher positions at the same rate. Sadly, equal levels of competence do not equate to equal treatment or promotional rates. Gender remains a part of the condition.

In 2005, the *Harvard Business Review* replicated a 1965 survey which gathered feedback about male and female executive attitudes towards women in leadership roles. The following table highlights the differences over a forty-year span:

Survey Question	1965	2005
Female favorable attitudes to-wards women in management	82 percent	88 percent
Male favorable attitudes towards women in management	35 percent	88 percent
Men being comfortable working for a women boss	27 percent	71 percent

A large percentage of men in the 1965 study had unfavorable attitudes towards women in management. Men in the 1965 study were also quoted as saying "[w]omen had a special place, which was outside the ranks of management." Societal prejudices against "women working outside the home" were also cited. Fortunately, 2005 attitudes have improved.

In 2010, Fox News stated that women "win elections at roughly equal rates with their male counterparts." Really? As of this writing, there are nine female governors in the United States. Twenty-two states have never had a female governor in the highest state office. And, just forty-four women have ever served in the high status position of governor. The District of Columbia and Guam are also currently governed by women. The United States, as we all know, has never had a female president or vice president. Barriers and biases are real.

Other studies suggest that Democratic women "represent more liberal, urban, racially diverse, and wealthier districts" than their Democratic male opponents. Pew Research Center's 2005 report found that public opinion "appears to favor more women in leadership." So, why aren't there more women leaders?

Overall, though, we are seeing notable shifts in attitudes towards women in management. In the past decades, there was an impressive drop in the proportion of men "who thought that a woman must be *exceptional* to succeed in business." This went from ninety percent in 1965 to an impressive thirty-two percent in 2005. Attitudes are changing.

A 2006 poll found significant differences in preferences for male and female bosses based on an employee's age. Going forward, these 2006 findings are predicted to continue to shift in favor of a preference for female bosses.

AGE	Preferred a male boss	Preferred a female boss
18 to 34	31 percent	29 percent
35 to 54	38 percent	19 percent
55 plus	40 percent	11 percent

According to a 2017 Gallup poll, in time, younger generations will not have stereotypical preferences for a male leader. The old school paradigm of "think manager, think male" is fading. But, let's remember that both men and women still use default language that uses "him" or predominantly masculine verbiage when talking about leadership and certain positions. For example, chairman of the board, councilman, firemen, and policemen are literally "male" terms. Think about a nurse, teacher, pilot, baker, and plumber. We quickly assign gender to those roles without really thinking about it.

When looking at gender and group composition, savvy voters should also be aware of the importance of communal versus traditional leadership characteristics. Ethics, authenticity, and servant leadership pertain to both women and men, and thus violate these expectations.

Furthermore, in leaderless group discussions, men who appeared more authoritative and exuded self-confidence had a distinct advantage. However, when the type of task expected of that leader was considered masculine (like mowing the lawn) or feminine (like taking care of the baby), gender and role assignment perceptions prevailed. Case in point, do you recognize this 2018 family photo?

The mother is the Prime Minister of New Zealand, Jacinda Ardern, with her partner, Clarke Gayford. Yes, a high status female political figure and a new mother. Stories about this "unique" situation actually flooded news channels; Ardern is actually only the second world leader to give birth while in office. News outlets even questioned her ability to run a country and breastfeed at the same time.

Women continue to face prejudices and stereotypes that men do not. "Many individuals, especially men, describe leaders in stereotypical terms that favor males over females" according to Powell (2011). Gender stereotypes are challenging to erase without time or direct intervention. Gradual changes have been documented, but not at the same rate that other issues have been tackled. More women attend and graduate college. More women are entrepreneurs. And, a handful are now CEOs of major corporations.

The default belief is that male leaders are taken for granted. We use this in our word choice and in our mental constructs. Bias against women in leadership is identified two ways: by agentic deficiency (not much political competence) and by agentic penalty (backlash for counter-stereotypical behaviors). Women are often called the more emotional sex, which places a constraining label on them that holds potentially damaging results. Gender stereotypes usually put women in vulnerable roles from which escape is difficult.

Without structure and routine, people usually retreat to personal biases and stereotypes regarding decision making. Likewise, people tend to go with something that is like themselves in terms of gender, philosophies, and social norms.

When looking at the complexity of a person poised for a prescribed leadership role, we consider appearance, social, cultural capital, and economic status to determine whether or not that person is fit for office. When we pick an individual who possesses valued social capital by the dominating class, this person is then granted access to additional resources, thereby reinforcing and strengthening this individual's status within the group. In terms of gender, a woman may only gain access to a social class if she has a degree of social capital, or the same childhood experiences.

Female leaders are expected to display both strong leadership qualities while also behaving "like a lady." It's a fine balance. And, of course, conflict makes for good television. The media is ripe with visual and audio clips ready to be aired and dissected. Down to every frame, a politician's body, words, and tone are scrutinized. Sadly, viewers do not hear a lot of commentary on what went well or what worked. Instead, we are smothered in scandals, missteps, errors, and critical commentaries. For many, it's like a feeding frenzy for what went amiss and then capitalizing on it.

Are you a male or female viewer and voter? The very basic answer to this determines how, in many situations, you handle gender dynamics. Study after study has confirmed that both men and women are impacted by gender roles and biases. Key findings from the scholars confirm that:

- Men usually had significant leadership roles starting in their early to mid-thirties. For women, this may have been delayed due to child-rearing and related responsibilities.
- Men take more personal credit for their successes than women according to survey response results.
- Professional associations afford men and women credibility and visibility, though these associations are more powerful and abundant for men.

Both genders see the value of networking to develop and maintain relationships for advancement. Both acknowledge the need for intentional self-promotion; however, women reported that they struggled more with this action. For example, men are taught to always shake hands during introductions. Women, not so much. Too often we see a quick wave of the hand, hug, or even a kiss to the cheek.

One study suggested that females took more risks than males when applying for promotions that male colleagues or applicants declined. This was considered risky for women as they potentially "stood out" from the pack for career advancement. Overcoming adversity was common to a female's story compared to a male's childhood challenges.

The male childhood experience, also known as one's habitus, is typically steep in leadership experiences. On the other hand, most females lack childhood experiences during which to try out leadership skills. Men also tend to learn leadership through trial and error compared to women who learn leadership skills on the job. Successful leaders' childhood habitus are important foundations for career building and advancement.

Recall October 1963 and little John-John playing in the Oval Office with his dad, President John F. Kennedy. John Jr., a young male, was afforded countless opportunities to explore, play, and learn under the caring direction of a successful leader. These repeated childhood experiences shaped John, Jr., and his success in politics, law, and journalism until his tragic death in 1999. Where was his older sister, Caroline, during these times?

John Kennedy Jr. playing in the Oval Office at the White House, Washington, DC, October 15, 1963.

Fitzsimmons and others (2014) provide details as to the causes and timing of gender disparity in high-level positions. Specifically, women are at a great disadvantage starting with negative or leadership limited childhood experiences (habitus) and continuing throughout their career. For many women:

Childhood	Junior Management	Middle Management	Executive Management
Directed to "traditional" tasks and roles	Sexual harassment	Assumption of having children; will leave anyway	Doesn't possess the required leadership confidence or resilience
Lack of career guidance	Lack of confidence in communicating success	Fear of reputational damage to mentors through sexual innuendo	Lack of visibility to board networks
Lack of access to non-traditional female role models	Less will to risk moving when faced with blockades	Lack of appropriate childcare/ partner support	Cultural stigma: "it's just the way it is"
Not permitted to engage in risky childhood play	Lack of advice, planning, and/or mentoring	Work structure prohibiting job sharing or part time	Doesn't possess appropriate leadership traits
Lack of access to team-based leadership activities	Not promoted to line roles	Won't put in the extra hours to show commitment	Lack of breadth and depth of experience relative to peers

A meta-analysis spanning a thirty-year time period found that men were favored over women in terms of salaries, bonuses, and promotions as evidenced by performance evaluations. Gender expectations hurt women from being universally perceived as having innate leadership potential. Minority women were subject to double jeopardy in facing both sexual and racial prejudices. Black and Hispanic women, based on research, are clustered in the lowest-earning occupations, including office and service jobs.

Women who also demonstrated agentic (masculine) qualities by showing competence were penalized for failing to align themselves with traditional communal (feminine) expectations. "Passive, emotional, and superficial" were used to stereotype women. Whereas, "assertiveness, tough, and decision-makers" were used to label male political leaders. Agentic labels like "achievement, competence, proficiency, and control" were assigned to men. Finding the balance of counter-stereotypes for men and women help or hurt a candidate's chance for success.

Voters do not readily assign female politicians positive qualities such as "experienced and knowledgeable." Strategies are important for when and how to use counter-stereotypes. By airing negative ads, female counter-stereotypical behaviors are judged.

Can a woman be both agentic in leadership while maintaining communal and family relationships? The expectations for each gender are quite different. Women have to jump two hurdles; one is their qualifications as a leader, and the other is their leadership style balancing agentic and communal traits.

Highly competent women at work also fall prey to female coworkers and subordinates via social backlashing. Research found that women won promotions when their effective behaviors aligned with desired female beliefs. The subset of caring for the individual as part of transformational leadership may give women an advantage over men for promotions. Women can use masculine traits to demonstrate fitness for leadership by acting on "firmness" and "competence," but some may read this as "cold and distant." There is always the risk of backlash. Taking care of both gender's needs is exhausting.

People who have bias against women pay close attention to leadership and gender differences and expectations. Meaning, how could or did "she" handle a political situation? A lack of female political leadership also plays into people's minds; often only male images emerge when thinking of a candidate or potential leader.

Females must be strategic as to not be "too" feminine or "too" masculine. For example, former Governor Sarah Palin was often described as "hot" or "pretty" during the 2008 presidential campaign. These feminine terms were not showered on Hillary Clinton.

For Clinton, her pantsuit choices were often analyzed along with trying to understand why she stayed in an unfaithful marriage to her husband. During the 2008 election, Palin was frequently praised for her figure, face, and youthful looking appearance. Many stories ran on her style of dress, as well. Below is an image of Palin at a Road to Victory Rally in Pennsylvania. Her style and appearance, and those boots, caught the eye of millions and countless news stories discussed this aspect along with her qualifications for office.

Whether perceived or real, hierarchy or status is assigned to men just by size. The height and muscle mass of a man are cues to his status. Height and muscle strength are aligned with physical dominance and naturally default to men.

The 2003 Bem Sex Role Inventory study examined sixty traits deemed feminine, masculine, or neutral in terms of how people define themselves. Categories included four different possible resulting categorizations: masculine, feminine, androgynous, and undifferentiated. Respondents looked at photographs and rated candidates using traits to which they were psychologically drawn. Republicans were viewed as masculine and Democrats were seen in feminine terms. These findings may impact voters especially when linked with gender expectations, stereotypes, and party affiliations. And, much of these are linked to body language and our expectations.

Female candidates "face a baseline disadvantage that varies across candidate gender and candidate partisanship" (Holman, 2016). Voters will select a female candidate when she is a part of that voter's political party, but still notice her gender more than her qualifications.

Gender bias can prevent women aspiring to be leaders from attaining and maintaining these positions. Women with lower voices who are larger in stature, between the ages of forty and sixty, and with higher levels of testosterone are favored.

Elizabeth Holmes, the founder and former CEO of Theranos, Inc. is a recent example of the power of a lower tone of voice. She was not only accused of conspiracy and fraud charges, but of intentionally using a lower (deeper) voice. Critics challenged the authenticity of her baritone voice and its varying pitch during different speaking engagements. This nonverbal element, along with her seemingly unblinking big eyes, received a lot of attention in the media; at times, almost surpassing her felony charges. Some even called her a sociopath based on her nonverbals.

Elizabeth Holmes speaks at Forbes Under 30 Summit at Pennsylvania Convention Center on October 5, 2015.

When men and women are placed into social roles with prescribed behaviors, gender stereotyping will continue and promote male-typical and female-typical roles. The "Queen Bee phenomenon" comes into play when women leaders in male-dominated fields distance themselves from more junior women in the organization which, in turn, perpetuates gender inequality. Isolation, I affirm, is the last thing women need in high status positions.

Women are punished for not being tough enough; yet, when they act "tough," they are also penalized for being manly or aggressive. In either case, the female is attacked for gender stereotype violations. When race is added to the gender mix, additional reactions to women leaders is exemplified.

Kosiara-Pedersen and Hanson (2014) suggest that "gender gaps in voting patterns might result from differences in ideological positions and policy opinions." Stereotyping and gender identifying apply to both sexes and also impact leadership perceptions.

Examining emotionally charged issues like education, crime, and abortion, Huddy and Terkildsen (1993) suggest that "competency expectations are most likely rooted in social stereotypes" specific to men and women.

Findings suggest that some voters are more apt to vote for a female when she plays to her gender trait expectations. If a female violates her expected characteristics, she may be condemned. Or, voters may attack her if she cannot "prove" she is masculine enough for the office. Cassese and Holman (2018) reference this as the "leaders, not ladies" imbalance. Group personality composition is also a factor considered for promoting or excluding women. The extraversion trait is important for the advancement of females.

US Department of Labor from 2014-15 statistics noted that the most common occupations for women in America included:

- Secretary/administrative assistant
- Elementary or middle school teacher
- Registered nurse, nursing, psychiatric, and home health aide
- First-time supervisor over retail salespersons
- Customer service representatives
- Domestic worker

Note that all of these occupations have a communal role including nurturing and caring for others. Women who have an "unequal share of domestic duties will be disadvantaged" according to Fitzsimmons, Callan, and Paulson (2014). Too often, women are guided towards careers that enable them to juggle domestic duties and support others.

Occupations and professions, especially those political in nature, are governed by rule makers who grant or restrict access. Access may be based on shared values or shared habitus mirror. *You are like me; therefore, I accept you into my group.* Apply this to political parties with shared constructs and individuals are either shunned or welcomed into a party. These deeply ingrained habits, skills, and dispositions are rooted in life experiences and extend to our lifestyle choices, as well.

Female priorities are usually community driven; yet, negative stereotypes and expectations for females hinder their abilities to be successful. We have gender expectations for political office and, too often, these biases impede our decision-making when promoting and voting for our public figures. Women are constantly judged if they are too masculine or too feminine.

For females to be considered effective, they need to show both sensitivity and strength. For male leaders, they only need to demonstrate strength. This double burden and unfair expectation is solely based on gender.

We want a leader who makes us feel valued as a part of something greater than ourselves. When issues around mortality and safety are the focus, a preference for a male leadership style emerges. During times of war, mortality, or the need to be tough, research confirms prejudice against female leaders. For example, while Hillary Clinton's 2016 "Fighting for Us" slogan was splashed across campaign stages, her demeanor was often photographed smiling, laughing, and having a good time. However, images like this are far from what we expect of a president who is "ready to fight."

Below, President Trump speaks during a 2018 campaign rally in Tennessee. His gestures, specifically his overt use of hands and arms, provide great information—regardless of what he is saying. Few argue that he is not entertaining to watch.

These gender stereotypes are "automatically activated and can be particularly damaging for women in leadership roles" during emotionally charged situations, like war. On the other hand, men are taught and expected to be agentic, possessing such qualities as decisiveness, independence, assertiveness, aggressiveness, and rationality. Whereas, women are labeled with more communal traits, including care for others, warmth, kindness, nurturer, and helper.

Task-framing is also a factor in that we assign gender to specific tasks and have expectations for how both genders should handle certain tasks. Luckily, research picked up on the female advantage when extroverted men had positive relationships with women. Needless to say, there is still a lot of work to be done to eradicate gender stereotypes. We've come a long way, but there is still a lot of progress to be made.

Do we present situations and opportunities that are gender-neutral? This should be taken into consideration by both genders. Most people, when you really think about it, are hesitant or resistant to change. It's not in our DNA, so we seek to maintain existing standards. This is in direct opposition to more free-thinking mind-sets. When we apply these mindsets to political labels, people tend to select the one which aligns with their inner thoughts, values, and belief systems.

Research confirms that conservative voters also have stricter expectations for women in office than liberal voters. One study even found that conservative women opposed, rather than supported, female candidates who aimed to shatter the glass ceiling.

Society's norm is that leadership is categorized as masculine; therefore, being a male leader is important. What positive male attributes can female candidates mirror that would shed light on their strengths without evoking negative perceptions from viewers? Four influential body language scenarios that women should do include:

1. **Stand up.** When women stand alongside men, the perception of equality is triggered. Too often, women remained seated in a mixed gender room which counters any message of strength. Those who show up, stand up.

2. **Be the leader at the head of the table.** Demonstrate status by physical location; flank others to the left and right.

3. **Step forward.** Stand out but still demonstrate feminine trait expectations. Speak well and control the environment.

4. **Look the part.** Match men's nonverbals. Make eye contact.

Being intentional with the use of one's prescribed gender or counter-stereotypical roles benefits both genders. However, females are still judged more harshly for their appearances, behaviors, actions, and the manner in which they present themselves.

Male candidates are not as strongly impacted by counter-stereotypes compared to females. Research found that men received less positive feedback when they adopted a 'less masculine' style. A male must still follow masculine roles while attempting to present a sensitive, vulnerable side.

Eight studies reviewed for this book focused on male and female politicians examined how respondents identified with gender-based traits. Specific traits for each gender included:

Feminine Traits	Masculine Traits
Affectionate	Assertive
Able to compromise	Able to handle a crisis
Cautious	Active
Sensitive	Coarse
Integrity	Knowledge
Emotional	Self-confident
Consensus-builder	Ambitious

Communal, feminine behaviors displayed by women had positive outcomes when combined with masculine behaviors. So, what does this mean? Again, it's confirmation that while women have made gains in political circles, gender expectations and perceptions are deeply rooted in us. We must use our brains and knowledge so as not to default or fault candidates solely on their gender.

News coverage also impacts voters' choices when candidate trait descriptions are included in the candidate profiles. Research confirms that traits and roles, when combined, impact gender perceptions. In turn, voting outcomes are impacted.

Gallup data from 2006 and 2017 was reviewed and the news is encouraging. Based on this longitudinal research study, roughly every ten to twenty years, a shift in how we view leadership gender is significantly changing. Specifically:

Year	Prefer a Male Boss	Prefer a Female Boss	No Preference
1953	68 percent	5 percent	25 percent
1977	62 percent	7 percent	29 percent
1993	47 percent	16 percent	35 percent
2001	49 percent	19 percent	31 percent
2017	23 percent	21 percent	55 percent

The preference for a male boss has continuously declined and the preference for a female boss has steadily increased. The category of no preference doubled between 1953 and 2017.

Studies also link masculinity and femininity to leadership perceptions. One cannot and does not overlook gender. When thinking of incredible leaders or envisioning the position of president, most people default to an image of a man in these roles. The traits people assign are masculine.

As the research clearly shows, it is obvious that appearances include gender biases and expectations. We must be keenly aware that these prescribed roles impact our voting decisions and that campaign strategies bank on this knowledge.

I suggest you first examine your preferences for a boss and leader. Do you default to a man or woman, based on what you see as the best fit for office? Can you only see the president as a man because you believe the role demands it? Take a moment to reflect on gender roles and expectations in America. Who are your role models? And, how do you punish other people who break, or challenge gender assigned roles? Do you remain silent, thereby agreeing, or do you speak up and challenge these deeply imbedded gender rules in each of us?

"Your silence will not protect you."
—Audre Lorde

CHAPTER 3

The Good, the Bad, and the Ugly: Labels and Stereotypes We Put on Others

Just as appearances matter, so do the labels we place on people and political parties. We must pay close attention to this during critical election years. We associate traits like competence, attractiveness, likability, trustworthiness, and value with someone who can secure the votes. And, we are subject to casting these traits onto anyone who belongs to a particular party, gender, race, age, and belief system.

In July 2019, presidential hopeful Senator Kirsten Gillibrand spoke to a group of voters in Ohio and was asked about white privilege, systemic racism, and how she would combat these divisive labels and conditions.

Gillibrand explained,

So institutional racism is real. It doesn't take away your pain or suffering. It's just a different issue. Your suffering is just as important as a black or brown person's suffering but to fix the problems that are happening in a black community you need far more transformational efforts that are targeted for real racism that exists every day.

But it doesn't mean that [doesn't] deserve my voice, lifting up your challenge. It also doesn't mean that black and brown people are left to fight these challenges on their own.

A white woman like me who is a senator and running for president of the United States has to lift up their voice just as much as I would lift up yours. That's all it means. It doesn't take away from you at all.

It just means we have to recognize suffering in all its forms and solve it in each place intentionally and with knowledge about what we are up against.

Though this is a book about body language and nonverbal communication, I challenge you to dissect Gillibrand's words and compare them to the research in this book. From color to gender, and titles to transformation, her use of emotional verbiage provokes us, one way or another.

For instance, you tell a group of people about something you read online. The subject is immigration and children being kept in substandard conditions. After a few moments, you get called a "bleeding heart." *What?* What triggered this label? It's rather simple—we tag people based on the feelings they chose to share. In turn, people react to certain topics or social issues and draw conclusions by assigning labels. As many know, "bleeding heart" can be a derogatory term for those who express politically liberal opinions. So, when you were called this, perhaps you were assigned to a political party who's affiliated with this label just by telling a story about a hot social issue. These are sensitive times, as we all know.

So what is a label? What is a stereotype? A blended definition is an "assignment to a category, especially inaccurately or restrictively," and "a widely held image or idea about a particular type of person or thing." If you agree with these basic definitions, then you agree that both have negative judgment implications. Additionally, labels and stereotypes are frequently used to describe politicians, candidates, political parties, issues, and campaigns—as well as those who support them.

Examples of political ideologies, views, labels and stereotypes for each party include:

Democrat	Republican
Liberal	Conservative
Progressives	Tea Party
Socialist movement	Freedom caucus
Left wing	Right wing
Socialists	Free market capitalism
Social liberalism	Social conservatives
Bleeding heart	Traditional values
Urban	Rural
Civil rights	Gun rights
Donkey	Elephant
Dems	GOP
Hippies	Elitists
Blue	Red
Feminists	Masculinists

With just the slightest bit of information, we assign labels or default to stereotypes. When we picture a person or a group, we "tend to fixate on prototypical characteristics and ignore other relevant information" (Ahler and Sood's, 2018). Our first or original thought of someone or something tends to stick with us, even when new, relevant information could change our thoughts and perceptions. Think of someone you met recently. How would you describe this person? By their appearance? Career? Gender? Race? Skill? Behavior? Of course. That's how it works. Labels define us.

Think about some presidents and think about their famous nickname labels. These labels trigger thought or feelings in us and visuals help to reinforce our perceptions of these leaders. In actuality, how honest was Abe? Who really liked Ike? Was Reagan that great of an orator? And, what made Nixon tricky?

Stereotyping is complex. It messes with our social and mental constructs. These viewpoints can help or hinder depending on the person and issue. This idea of a particular type of person or thing can impair our social and cognitive performance. Holding a stereotype also has a psychological and physiological impact on our brains and bodies. When our fixed mindsets are challenged, stress harms our working memory and emotional responses are triggered. Our stress is visually obvious.

Supported by first impression data, we make judgments about people in just a few seconds. As soon as we meet someone, we notice traits like aggressiveness, trustworthiness, likability, attractiveness, and competence. One study found that we can give a "yes" or "no" to these five traits in less than three seconds. So, traits targeting candidates, politicians, leaders, and those with certain ideologies would also be judged quickly. This is especially true for judgments involving our feelings. We slap on a label or mentally cross-reference our belief system to perpetuate the stereotype or challenge it.

We also tend to be partisan-homogeneous, like-minded consumers; we seek out and are attracted to those who are similar to ourselves. Politically speaking, many of us simply adopted our parents' political views or party as teens or young adults with little or no information about the expectations and beliefs of each party.

Over time and with new information, we either reaffirmed our beliefs, changed them, or disengaged altogether.

Stereotypes and prejudices are active practices according to the literature. It is important to look at situational cues which signal threat, the factors that heighten or reduce threat, and the consequences of such threats. Stereotyping is weakened when people have clear behavioral information for which to judge against their leader.

Visual bias creates and perpetuates stereotypes in the media. In turn, strong viewer responses are generated. Stereotyping and how it impacts us is rooted in the source of the threat and the target of the threat. Who said it and whom was it meant for? It can be blatant or subtly biased. Regardless, we know that there are consequences for deviating from one's prescribed labels and stereotypes.

For example, "Real men don't cry." Actually, they do. In 2017, Vice President Joe Biden wept when awarded the Presidential Medal of Freedom. There are numerous other cases of influential male politicians openly crying in public as well.

When we do not have objective or fact-based information, our default to appearance-based traits is normal. We must remember the power of what we see and how it aligns with our prescribed belief systems. I suggest we keep our eyes—and minds—open, so as to not fall into these traps, particularly when picking leaders and standing up for what we believe in.

How do we learn the traits and expectations about each political party? By definition, a "political party" cannot be understood first-hand; literally, we cannot meet "the party." In fact, we learn about our party choices from trusted friends and family, social media, personal experiences, and from consuming information about its people or ide-ologies. A lot of the time it's simple. First, look at someone; second, identify recognizable traits; and third, assign labels and stereotypes.

It's hard to digest that Michael and Susumu (2016) actually found that fifty-five percent to sixty-two percent of party affiliation was predicted just by looking at photos! People picked images that "looked the part." This could lead to some profound implications as voters select their leader or favorite candidate without one consider-ation of qualifications or experience. Overall, what people inferred from only looking at a face hindered the quality of their political choices. And research has confirmed that people made these judg-ments in less than one second. I recall many conversations over the years where the statement, "he (or she) doesn't look presidential enough" was uttered with confidence.

The media also perpetuates gender stereotypes. For example, Prime Minister Theresa May's favorite brands were printed in the *Telegraph* when she took office, but Tony Blair's fashion flairs went unmentioned throughout his term. Chancellor Angela Merkel's clothing choices for events frequently make the headlines. New Zealand Prime Minister Jacinda Ardern was asked how she could handle being a new mother in addition to running a country. (Her response was quite direct and is posted to her Facebook page. I recommend you check it out as well as subsequent posts from her followers.) Rarely do we see media hounds slinging such domestic issues towards men in power.

When women refrain from running due to brutal public judgments and media attacks, gaps in gender representation persist and women fall behind on the political landscape. Too often, behavior for women is judged against what is socially acceptable as "feminine" without considering other important qualifications like experience, personality, and ethics.

Stereotyping in commercials and social media has the ability to undermine those in leadership roles. Aligned with agentic and communal stereotypes, one study found a large gap between male and female candidates regarding media coverage. Female candidates' personal lives were the focus, while for male candidates, this was not the case. Hillary Clinton may have summed it up best: "If I want to knock a story off the front page, I just change my hairstyle." Seriously, people.

Gender stereotypes are defined as "carrying beliefs about appropriate behaviors for each sex" (Mavin, Bryans, and Cunningham, 2010). Gender is how individuals interact with each other, with specific expectations in social situations. Gender stereotyping and British leaders were the source of one study in the United Kingdom. Labels about politicians that were splashed by the British media included Blair's Babes, Gordon's Gals, Cameron's Cuties, and Nick's Nymphets. For these male leaders, they were stereotyped as men with adorning females. Ridiculous, sexist, and offensive.

"Stereotyping or assigning characteristics to political leaders of a certain group is largely gender based" and voters tend to "show a preference for stereotypically masculine traits over feminine characteristics when determining who should hold high office." (Huddy and Terkildsen, 1993).

Stories about appearance, dress, hair, and style are frequently the subject of British women in power. From color and fit, to frequency of being worn, media hounds keep score of a woman's heels, hair, and style. Headlines about Duchess Kate Middleton often ramble on about her dress choices. Talk of her physical body, age, skin, curves, and style make the news on a regular basis. There is a fine balance between dressing per one's prescribed gender role and going overboard. This is not the same for men. When a female gives attention to her appearance, she is judged based on these choices far more than men's selection of a suit and tie.

Unfortunately, "gender biases do not transcend political parties." Regardless of political affiliation, a man is supposed to act like a man and a woman is supposed to be ladylike. Adult men are usually called men. Adult women are often called girls.

In leadership, gender-assigned traits are at play and are continuously judged to confirm stereotypes or challenge via counter-stereotypes. Genetic penalties, also called social backlash, result from acting against one's prescribed role. Backlash happens more often and more harshly for women who stray from their gender-driven roles. Men experience this to a lesser degree. The traditional male role includes task-oriented masculine traits. For women, femininity includes communal (relational) traits.

A rather exhaustive list of expected leadership labels and their actions/behaviors includes:

LABELS	ACTION/BEHAVIOR
Agreeableness	Cooperative, agreeable, thoughtful, considerate
Antagonism	Disagrees, aggressive, seems unfriendly
Authoritarianism	Dominance, authoritative
Conscientiousness	Control, regulate, and direct one's impulses
Creativity	Imagination, innovative, idea-driven, experimentation
Emotional stability	Freedom from hypersensitivity, emotional maturity
Extraversion	Talkative, outgoing, makes jokes, asks questions, gives opinions
Femininity	Gender role and characteristics of women

LABELS	ACTION/BEHAVIOR
Intelligence	Numerical aptitude, average grade in college, scholastic achievement, cognitive complexity, analytical thinker
Leadership experience or potential	Supervisory aptitude, motivation to lead, past leadership experience, visible, future success as a leader, initiative, group goal commitment, individual goals for the group
Masculinity	Masculine, gender role
Neuroticism	Shows tension, tense, sensitive
Openness to experience	Innovative, imaginative, creative, open to experience
Self-esteem	Confidence in one's own worth; self-respect
Self-efficacy	Belief in the ability to achieve goals and execute courses of action
Social Skills	Friendliness, gives information, sensitive, listener, gives suggestions

Of these fifteen labels, research found that five were predictors for leadership emergence. They included:

√ **Authoritarianism**
√ **Creativity**
√ **Extraversion**
√ **Masculinity**
√ **Intelligence**

Think back to individuals or leaders who have seared images in your brain. Do any of these qualities match her or him? For example, do you see the masculine label of authoritarianism in this photo of US Attorney General William Barr? Or, do you see the feminine label of conscientiousness based on Barr's controlled facial expression and body position?

Do see you former Secretary of State, Condoleezza Rice, as an agreeable feminine label? Or, as an intelligent (masculine) female based on her high-status role and position at the podium?

Gender does play a role, consciously or subconsciously, in job role expectations, particularly in the role of president of the United States and other high-ranking leaders who guide our country. Republicans are usually stereotyped as conservative with traditional family values, including gender-based expectations. For Democrats, labels include non-traditional, change agents, radicals, and pot stirrers for challenging the value system and traditions of our nation. For those tackling hot topics like abortion, alternative lifestyles, and addressing income disparities, we might also see feel-good labels like tree hugger environmentalists and social radicals in the mix.

Bernie Sanders pumps his fist after speaking to a crowd of supporters at a Democratic unity rally at the Rail Event Center on April 21, 2017 in Salt Lake City.

One case in point, when 2016 Democratic candidate Senator Bernie Sanders embarked on a demanding campaign circuit, his physical actions (including fist pumps and pursed lips) and seemingly passionate, or aggressive, presentation style came under scrutiny. Democratic Party affiliates quickly labeled him as a socialist or, in the very least, inferred it. The fear that our country could fall under socialist rule was enough for many older Americans to shy away from supporting him. Of course, the power of perceptions, laden with reinforcing stereotypes, is perpetuated by new stories, video and image clips, and the never-ending stream of journalist commentaries.

The appearance of a candidate and how we vote have a connection. Both men and women candidates are vulnerable to media attacks on policy issues associated with their respective genders and party affiliations. But Democratic women fare the worst according to Cassese and Holman's (2018) findings. And, we viewers and voters are absolutely subject to media's whims and ways. Even within Republican and Democratic parties, men and women succumb to expected stereotypes.

Republicans believe that their party men are better at handling crime issues. They are perceived to be tough on crime. Almost thirty-five percent of Republicans state that Republican men can handle issues of crime better than Republican women. This stands in contrast to the fourteen percent of Democratic men who think Democratic women can handle crime. (Cassese and Holman, 2018)

Perceptions are powerful and deeply connected to our views of other people and their political party affiliations. Based on Ahler and Sood's (2018) research on political party perceptions, people believed that thirty-two percent of Democrats were LGBTQ (lesbian, gay, bisexual, transgender, and questioning—or queer). In reality, only six percent identified with this category. People also thought that thirty-eight percent of Republicans earned more than $250,000 per year. In truth, it's only two percent.

On the heated issue of abortion, results were similar specific to political party and women. However, Republican women were punished more frequently compared to Republican men and Democratic women. Certain attributes, both negative and positive, impact an individual's emergence as a leader.

Emergent leadership requires dominance, empathy, independence, intelligence, self-efficacy, self-monitoring, and verbal expression. Individual prominence, group goal facilitation, group sociability, physical energy (initiative), IQ, and emotional stability are also valued.

The "halo effect" also has an impact on political prediction rates. How the candidate looks has a significant impact on how the most uninformed people will vote. We know the power of the halo effect on judging individual attributes. Think about this in terms of how a leader is villainized or sensationalized.

Russian President Vladimir Putin gives a speech during the Tsinghua University ceremony at Friendship Palace on April 26, 2019 in Beijing, China.

Do we see beady little eyes with a smirk on his mouth as someone plotting against us with threats of nuclear war? Or, do we a see confident world leader leaning in and taking notice of his surroundings and people in the room?

North Korean leader Kim Jong-un.

Do we see a jovial young man smiling at his guests? Or, do we see a gluttonous dictator enjoying the opulence of his wealth at the expense of his suppressed people? Do we judge these faces as ones ready to deceive us? Absolutely. Because we just have enough information on Russia's President, Vladimir Putin, and North Korea's Supreme Leader, Kim Jong-un.

Regardless of what you think and feel about these two world leaders, much has also been said about their looks. Putin has even been photographed riding shirtless on a horse to highlight his physique. When it comes to the definition of beauty, there are cues that cross cultures of how individuals agree and judge what is attractive. How challenging this must be for the overqualified candidate who isn't good-looking based on society's definition of beauty. With a simple search, you'll find millions of results for the hot, sexy, best looking, and attractive leaders throughout history. Are you shaking your head in disbelief? I doubt it.

In addition to the agreed-upon appearance labels and pre-scribed stereotypes most of us adhere to, traits and behaviors like masculinity, femininity, intelligence, and dominance are considered specific to our perceptions of leadership. During face-to-face interactions, we also watch for extraversion and emotional stability. These factors emanate through the body and speak volumes without uttering a word!

Certain emblems worn by leaders label them a particular way. For example, we notice when a candidate is wearing or not wearing the American flag pin. We expect male politicians to wear solid, bold red or blue ties. We expect candidates to appear on stages wearing red, white, and blue clothing while standing in front of a line-up of waving flags. We take notice if we see a yarmulke on someone's head. If these conditions and others like them are violated, we quickly ask ourselves, where's their loyalty to our country? Overall, we adorn our bodies like billboards to let others know where we stand.

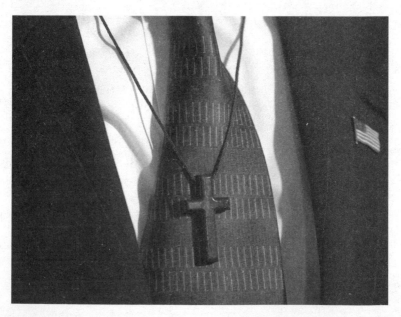

Of course, emblems and labels are not limited to just the United States or to politicians. Many recognize various people or groups by their emblems. To name a few:

What we see:	Who we think of:
Swastika	Nazis
Peace symbol	Hippies
Cross	Christian
Star of David	Jewish
Hijab	Muslim woman
Hammer and sickle	Communism

Individual and conceptually distinct labels required of leaders, both emerging and current, included traditional personality traits like extraversion and emotional stability in addition to social and intelligent. Ensari and others (2011) concluded that, "Men who appear Authoritarian and who are self-confident (and extroverted/ socially skilled) have a distinct advantage." Appearance is key to that finding, in my opinion.

Visual images that communicate something about people are not just limited to clothing, emblems, gender, and political parties. We also see and judge color. In particular, skin color. The intersectionality of these traits, labels, and stereotypes suggest that oppression is a result of gender and racial inequalities.

One study targeting racial stereotypes found that when the stereotype of "African American as less intelligent" was "in the air" and subtly hinted to people in a classroom, black students underperformed compared to their white peers on standardized tests.

In another study based on one's work environment, black women who made mistakes were "penalized more severely" than black men and white women leaders. This "two-degrees removed" status from the white male stereotypical leadership profile harmed minority women. Heck, it would damage even the most confident professional. Asian women faced the double jeopardy stereotype, as well. Yet, their situation tended to fall into the "dual identity" category in that one trait was noticed or judged before the other trait. This is different than intersectionality.

Racial images in advertising most often take the form of implicit verses explicit verbal appeals. Advertising manipulations include darkening the skin tone of non-white people to trigger a negative emotion, or including vulnerable people, like children, in war-like conditions. These are intentional and they perpetuate stereotypes.

Most research confirms that black candidates fall short of their white counterparts based on the use of color in advertising. McIlwain and Caliendo (2009) found that white voters were "more likely to attribute positive characteristics to white candidates over black candidates." And, some studies suggested that African Americans are prototypically Democrat. Just by their skin color, and with no other information, black people were defaulted to a particular party.

Other alarming studies found that minority female stereotypes included:

- Angry, dominant black women
- Quiet, reserved, shy, mild-tempered, and intellectual Asian women
- Intellectual, communal white women

Specific to behavior, black women were stereotyped as "having an attitude," "being loud," "confident," and "assertive." Asian women were also stereotyped as "quiet" and "family-oriented." White women in the study were viewed as "arrogant," "rich," and "ditzy."

In terms of perceived competence, black women were viewed as "dominant, but not competent." Asian women were "competent, yet passive." And, white women were "communal but not dominant or excessively competent." This particular study found that black women may fare the best because their stereotyping aligned closest to the agentic (masculine) traits required of leaders. Even though darker skinned candidates were judged as less experienced and intelligent based on Weaver's (2012) study, they were labeled as having "a greater work ethic and greater trustworthiness."

Diving deeper into studies on women and color, very specific stereotypes were noted based on a woman's physical appearance, behavior, intellect, strengths, and negativities. These labels included:

Black women	Asian women	White women
Bossy	Slow to anger	Pretty
Aggressive	Laid back	Beautiful
Quick to anger	Calm	Youthful
Overbearing	Quiet	Good looking
Loud	Reserved	Attractive
Boisterous	Shy	Kind
Unruly	Smart	Caring
Erratic	Intelligent	Team-minded
Annoying	Wise	Kind-hearted
Frustrated	Educated	
	Knowledgeable	
	Healthy	
	Lucky	
	Petite	

The work of Messing and others (2016) found that, when participants were exposed to candidates with varying skin colorations, stereotypical and often negative affective responses towards black people were documented. Labels tagged to black women are extremely negative; however, they are more closely aligned with masculine or agentic behaviors expected of leaders. If this is the case, then black female candidates fare better on the campaign trail and in voting booths compared to white female candidates.

When women were threatened with the stereotype of men being better leaders, many shifted their own styles to adapt and present a more masculine style. But this has a social cost in that others viewed them as less warm and not as likable. Simply adopting male behaviors in difficult situations is not necessarily the answer. However, a favorable outcome was found in a study when the stereotype was addressed head on and challenged. Women were able to react against it and outperform their male counterparts. Reasons for this may also include buffering, role models, and reducing threatening situations.

However, the very fact of being female and all of the stereotypes that are associated with this gender continue to inhibit their ability to secure high-ranking political positions. Candidates may be judged harshly when media attacks infer that the candidate has violated a stereotype about them (or their group). Part of this expectancy violation theory suggests that female candidates remain more vulnerable to trait-based attacks specific to feminine stereotypes. And, these attacks actually start in childhood.

Research findings from male and female childhood habitus (experiences) found that those in high level positions (like CEO or perhaps president) shared similar childhood experiences in addition to having unique experiences solely based on their gender.

Criterion	Unique to Male	Shared	Unique to Female
Family structure	Family life was "traditional" and "settled"	Attributed strong work ethic to the role of the father	Female family member played a critical role, such as the aunt or grandmother who went beyond a domestic role

Prominent family figure	Encouraged by the father to attend college	Deemed father's value system to be ethical	Demonstrated that one could achieve both business and family goals without sacrificing either
Education	School coaches and male teachers seen a role models	School played a prominent role	Told that "girls could do anything" built self-efficacy
Early work	Work enabled them to test and experiment with leadership	Part-time work was important	Gained independence, but learned family business stewardship
Significant experiences	Generally not disruptive	N/A	Negative significant event (family death, abuse, violence)
Leadership through team sport	Almost all reported that this was significant	N/A	N/A
Mentors	N/A	Contributed to growing leadership, humility and courage	N/A
Networking	N/A	Critical for career advancement and maintenance	N/A

(N/A – Study did not include specific information for this criterion)

The role of a CEO and the role of president share similarities. They tend to be non-routine, unstructured, idiosyncratic, and complex. These leaders are required to have a proven track record of being a successful strategist with high levels of intelligence, in addition to possessing self-confidence and integrity with regard to taking care of the team. This paramount position impacts every person within the structure and how the system performs as a whole. I suggest, as a country, we cautiously and critically watch, study, and learn about each candidate vying for the office of president.

For women, a significant childhood disruption was often reported. From death or illness of family members to domestic violence or teenage estrangement, females reported having to take on an adult role during their teen years. Yet, women attributed this to developing "inner strength," "strength of character," or "self-efficacy."

For men, childhood male activities often included camping, fishing, hiking, working on cars, and playing team sports. These team events allowed males to learn lessons about integrity, courage, leadership, strategy, and self-efficacy. These physical sports served males well—perhaps by preparing them for conflict or demonstrating physical strength during stressful and competitive conditions.

Women, on the other hand, tend to distance themselves during times of threat. There is a sense of self-worth attached to this action. By disengaging during challenging situations, a female may seek to self-preserve. However, this comes at a price in that it can lead to performance challenges, perceptions of motivation, and failure to associate with the group altogether. Without a sense of belonging, women may suffer negative self and professional outcomes.

Research suggests that the stereotypical traits of leadership are masculine and agentic. Regardless, the default result is the selection of a male leader under mortally salient conditions. Meaning, when we perceive harm or threat, we default to a male for help. Think of the classic knight in shining armor trope.

When death or the thought of harm is a part of the formula, people respond by selecting leaders aligned with cultural gender stereotypes. Studies found a preference for male leadership and a decreased preference for female leadership during these times. Part of this prejudice included the agentic gender traits assigned to leaders, and these same agentic traits assigned to men but not women.

Vice Chief of Naval Operations Admiral Michelle Howard participates in a news conference about a series of reforms to the troubled nuclear force at the Pentagon.

For example, when you look at four-star Admiral Michelle Janine Howard, do you emotionally and intellectually believe she can command a Navy ship under war-time conditions? And, once you have processed the fact that she once served as commander of US Naval Forces Europe, commander of US Naval Forces Africa, and commander of Allied Joint Force Command Naples, how do you feel about her being the first African American women to command a US Navy ship? Proud? Shocked? Amused? Secure in the belief that she would kill in order to save you?

Stereotypes marginalize both genders, and electoral systems influence how voters vote and how each gender is perceived. Female candidates must blend and balance masculine traits associated with leadership, while maintaining prescribed feminine characteristics to gain acceptance. This is simply a catch-22. Females also tend to be associated with being more liberal than men, thereby making them less popular with conservatives. Overall, women remain stereotyped as "compassionate, warm, and kind;" men are stereotyped as "assertive, tough, and competent."

Even though "on average, women in national legislature across the world increased from twelve percent in 1997 to twenty-four percent in 2018," women political leaders "still face issues challenges that their male counterparts do not" (Liu, 2019). "Gender inequality and parity in political institutions are unlikely to be achieved unless gender norms around the role of women in society are eliminated. Such work can only be done in a collective effort by the general public, the media, political parties, and others." This is easier said than done.

Society tends to default social issues like welfare, childcare, and family issues to women. We know there are significant differences in domestic roles for women and men and how these roles impact careers and choices. While many female leaders have children, most still assume the primary domestic role in addition to their high-status job. Many, however, report that their spouses have supportive and active domestic responsibilities.

A growth mindset from both genders must exist in order to tackle gender stereotypes. Without the belief that someone can grow, learn, and change, women may be stuck "in the kitchen" or men will continue to "babysit" their own children—both are unhealthy psychological mindsets.

By creating a buffer between real or perceived threat labels, women can become empowered and mindsets subsequently will shift. In cultivated leadership capabilities, women with high levels of self-efficacy and self-esteem will do better and be more mentally prepared for agentic and demanding leadership tasks. By shielding damaging stereotypes, things can change.

For example, in one study, women were led to believe that traditional male tasks such as negotiating and leadership could be developed. In turn, women were able to successfully react against the negative stereotype that women were, in fact, inferior in a "man's world." Hoyt and Murphy (2016) continue to remind us that, "[n]egative stereotyping has been shown to lead to women's underperformance on negotiation tasks, managerial and leadership tasks." There are severe consequences with stereotyping, including vulnerability, performance, disengagement, and misidentification solely based on gender.

Cues include sexist remarks, or hints of sexuality that linger "in the air" long after the words have left the room. When someone is the "token" for being in the numerical minority, feelings of isolation explode. By being "the only" in a group, defensive response mechanisms are triggered and, too often, are detrimental.

These can be particularly damaging for women in the political spotlight. In situations in which there is competition, negative stereotypes harm females in that they may not be able to "stand the heat." Or, perhaps they need to "toughen up." In many traditionally male-dominated fields, this is evident as women continue to shy away from applying or engaging in opportunities.

Women will also be less verbally fluent, use more tentative language, and shift their decisions under the rotting spell of negative stereotyping. A sense of belonging and connectedness are important for people's motivations and achievement in all fields and social situations. "In traditional male fields, women often face 'belonging uncertainty'" (Hoyt and Murphy, 2016). No doubt that "stereotype threat can undermine women in leadership."

Leadership roles for women run the gamut of being wildly successful or phenomenally devastating. When we present a situation or condition and assign gender expectations for both people and tasks, confidence, value, contribution, and performance are all impacted.

Good news, though. Evidence of gender-based leader stereotypes are changing. By having a more androgynous view of leadership, we chip away at centuries-old thinking. When the media puts women in counter-stereotypical roles, research finds that women report stronger nontraditional role beliefs, less negative self-perceptions, and higher leadership aspirations when compared to stereotypical roles.

Research confirms that women in leadership are more trans-formational then men. They also typically rate higher in all of the dimensions of transformational leadership, including charisma, inspirational motivation, intellectual stimulation, and considera-tion for the individual.

We also know that the type of leadership style expected of a high status candidate is important. All three—transformational leadership, transactional leadership, and laissez-faire leadership—come with prescribed expectations from both genders.

Transformational leaders exhibit charisma, inspiration, intel-lectual stimulation, and individual consideration. Meaning, they communicate with their followers, are excited about the mission or purpose, encourage questions and new perspectives, and focus on needs through mentoring and modeling. Think about the communal or caring mindset associated with this style; it tends to be feminine.

Transactional leaders exhibit contingent reward and manage-ment by exception. Meaning, followers are rewarded for doing their assigned tasks while being monitored or supervised by the leader. These leaders intervene to manage problems but wait until these are brought to their attention. Contingent rewards focus on the task at hand and rewards high performance while punishing bad performance. These attributes lean towards the masculine gender role and stereotype.

Laissez-faire leaders, overall, avoid the responsibilities expected of leadership. They fail to give direction and do not engage with follower development or morale. Too often, we have seen this hands-off, failure to take responsibility approach in many leader-ship positions. Victimizing, finger pointing, and blame game tac-tics followed by literal shrugs of "I don't know" or "Not me" are witnessed.

Specific to the roles associated with transactional leadership, women were found to be rated higher in the contingent reward dimension. Men received higher markings for active management by exception and passive management. In regard to laissez-faire leadership, men typically scored higher than women.

We also know that role models can be both helpful and harmful for women by either protecting them from stereotypical types or adding to their feelings of inadequacy. One study found that women felt "deficient" compared to other highly successful women if the relationship was not properly nourished. On the other hand, female role models have the ability to protect women and aid in their self-ratings of competence and confidence.

While gender beliefs are specific to how both men and women should behave, prescriptive gender stereotypes are quite specific as to how each should behave. These prescriptive beliefs pertain to ideal or desirable attributes for men and women.

Prescriptive gender stereotypes for how men and women should lead and behave include assertiveness and being direct for men, and sensitivity and caring for women. There is evidence that, in general, people perceive women as less successful than their male peers. Aligned with stereotypical gender roles, women leaders tend to be stereotyped as more democratic and less autocratic.

Types of jobs were also associated with gender role assignment. Specifically, men were considered to be more effective in military settings and women were found to be better in education, social service, and government work. In business settings, neither sex prevailed. We must be aware that workplaces have subtle forms of discrimination, which have negative outcomes for women leaders. For example, does a boss subconsciously groom a female leader for a people-centric, communal position, or for a demanding, analytical role? One study found that men were more effective in lower level management roles and women were more effective in middle level management positions where people skills tended to have higher value.

Gender stereotyping is the source of many dysfunctional systems in our leadership, including government. Too often, the masses believe that women are less competent for leadership. And, when women rise to higher level positions, their leadership is often questioned and, at times, deemed illegitimate according to many studies. In turn, the threat of being stereotyped as "incompetent damages women's leadership performance and aspirations" (Eagly and Heilman, 2016).

The "glass cliff" effect also causes damage. When women's access to high level leadership positions that are inherently risky and ultimately prone to fail, results can be devastating. Not only are these fragile positions ripe with unique challenges based on the position itself, but the expectations required of its leaders are unique. When females are promoted to these positions, additional risk factors for failure emerge.

Female-based powerless actions and behaviors also include sexual harassment, violence against women, and lack of productive freedom. Research on and advocacy of these topics remain heated, and it evokes strong feelings from both men and women. On campaign trails and during political debates, candidates spend countless hours trying to convince us that their ideologies align with our standards and that by voting for them, our voices will be heard.

People use gender to make inferences specific to a candidate's ideologies, traits, and belief systems. And, "once women take on leadership positions, they incur an agentic penalty for exhibiting behavior that it too agentic and that contradicts prescribed gender stereotypes" (Rosette et al., 2016).

Research suggests that women in government trigger sexist attitudes. Strengths and weaknesses are perceived based on candidates' gender, but target females more than males. Men are understood to handle America's tough issues like crime, the military, and the economy; women are typecast to handle compassion-like issues, including education, poverty, and health care.

Gender traits for both sexes can have both positive and negative connotations. For example, if a woman is decisive and tough, she fails to have compassion and may not compromise. For a man, if he exhibits warmth and kindness, he may be seen as unable to handle difficult situations. In plain terms, he is weak.

This also pertains to trait stereotypes for females. Most females fall within the terms of beautiful, warm, and caring, but leadership traits are rarely used to describe a female in politics. While male politicians are considered a subgroup of being male, this is not the case for females in politics. Female politicians are different than just being a female.

Schneider and Bos (2014) do an excellent job summarizing gender-specific qualities by highlighting stark gender differences based on the four dimensions of personality, thought, and physical appearance. The table highlights the stereotypes associated with each gender.

Trait	Women	Men
Positive personality	Affectionate, gentle, sensitive, and sympathetic	Daring, adventurous, competitive, and aggressive
Negative personality	Gullible, whiny, fussy, and nagging	Hostile, greedy, boastful, and egotistical
Cognitive (thoughts)	Artistic, creative, and imaginative	Analytical, quantitatively skilled, and problem solver
Physical	Pretty, beautiful, and gorgeous	Rugged, muscular, and physically strong

Findings noted that female personality traits found women to be warm, but whiny, or gentle, yet nagging. For males, tough was a plus; however, egotistical was not in their favor. When looking at these expected traits, female politicians struggle to fit in with either group. Research found gaps in characteristics between women and businesswomen, and women versus female managers based on observed behaviors or traits expected of the leadership role. One study noted that "female politicians were perceived to have twice as many 'negative female leader traits' as professional women" (Schneider and Bos, 2014).

When female politicians were compared to female professionals, stereotypical female traits were assigned to the professionals, but not to the politicians. A subset of this study looked at female politician, male politician, and politician traits in which participants selected specific traits to each. The following table captures the notable difference in female politician traits compared to expected politician traits. Note the close scores between male politicians and expected political traits.

Trait	Female Politician	Male Politician	Politician Expectation
Educated	68 percent	92 percent	90 percent
Well-educated	64 percent	82 percent	81 percent
Competitive	62 percent	82 percent	86 percent
Ambitious	58 percent	84 percent	79 percent
Aggressive	49 percent	71 percent	81 percent

Female politicians, on the other hand, struggled with being labeled as either feminine or masculine. Other studies found that female politicians did not possess leadership, competence, and masculine characteristics compared to male politicians.

Researchers also found that three traits (ambition, drive, and assertiveness) were identified as positive traits for male politicians, but negative for female leaders. This is commonly called the "double bind" in which one trait works for one gender but penalizes the other. Looking at the two charts below, some glaring biases emerge. First, the terms used to describe women vary significantly from the labels assigned to men. Additionally, female politicians were rated lower based on their prescribed roles; whereas, political men received higher marks.

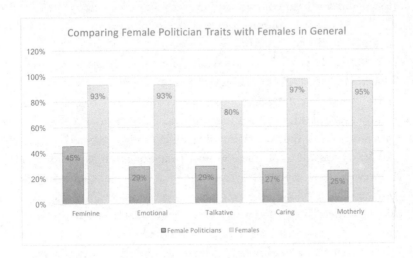

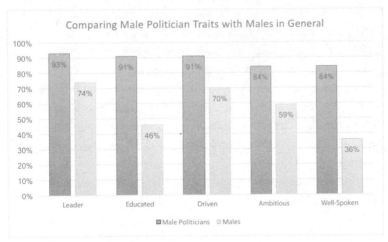

Schneider and Box (2014)

Additionally, female politicians' top traits included: well-educated, confident, assertive, well-spoken, and hardworking. This is in contrast to women without the political reference whose traits included: sensitive, beautiful, compassionate, affectionate, and loving. In general, traits associated with women in politics or women in business significantly varied from women without other stereotypes.

For men, expectations and trait assignment also varied from male politicians compared to men only.

For male politicians, top traits included: charismatic, well-spoken, leader, and well-educated. For men only, highest ranked traits included: competitive, masculine, independent, and strong. Educated and leader tied for the top five. Participants believed that men, in general, should exhibit physically strong characteristics but did not necessarily apply these same expectations to male politicians. However, a few traits did overlap for male politicians and men in general. "Men find male party leaders more knowledgeable than female leaders" according to Kosiara-Pedersen and Hansen (2014). One study using identical politically-themed résumés labeled with male or female names found that male candidates were considered having "greater political skill and potential" than female candidates. Remember, these were identical except for the names.

The lack of fit model also pigeonholes women specific to gender stereotyping and job discrimination. Studies confirm that women who seek male-dominated professions face uphill battles in terms of perceived fitness for the position. This is only because of one factor—gender. A woman is not fit because she is a woman. Honestly, I know this sounds insane, but in reality, some people believe this.

Stereotyping impacts gender, level of office vacancy, media coverage, candidate strategies, voter bias, voter external influences, and preconceived cognitive constructs of what is right, just, and fair. Stereotyping happens to both genders and also includes a host of other demographic features such as attractiveness, health, age, education, and ethnicity.

One gender and political party analysis yielded interesting, but not surprising, results based on how each gender would handle three hot issues: education, crime, and abortion. Almost 700 participants in the study answered the question, "Who would do a better job in the US Congress handling __(issue)__, a Democratic/

Republican man or woman?" Note that an option for equally good or bad was also included in the study. Below is a summary:

Issue:	Education	Education	Crime	Crime	Abortion	Abortion
Party:	Democratic Politicians	Republican Politicians	Democratic Politicians	Republican Politicians	Democratic Politicians	Republican Politicians
Men were better at:	5.1	4.3	**18.5**	**19.7**	9.4	9.8
Women were better at:	**24.6**	**23.9**	6.4	5.9	**40.7**	**33.0**

Overall, stereotyping disparities remained intact; women were considered better at handling education and abortion topics, whereas men were better with crime issues. Almost half of respondents believed that gender played a role on how abortion would be handled. Also, Democratic women were viewed as more liberal than Democratic men specific to the abortion issue.

Researchers also received a myriad of variables about each gender, including age, education, race, party affiliation, and political knowledge. These were then compared against the three issues of education, crime, and abortion. Findings suggested that:

1. Political knowledge predicted Democratic gender stereotypes, but not for Republican politicians.
2. Gender stereotypes yielded different outcomes between the two parties.
3. Republican women reviewed the harshest scores from respondents.

Perhaps Republican women scored poorly based on the double message that being female makes you liberal but being Republican makes you conservative. Which wins?

Based on the literature, the following gender-based findings should make all of us stand up and take notice. These are important, but too often, we gloss over their significance:

- Voters see gender within both parties.
- Females in executive roles may shift gender stereotypes.

- As adults, women tend to enter the political arena later in life.
- When asked, females state that their "families take precedence over their careers."
- Males are more likely to support a candidate who looks like them.
- Management is male according to the stereotype.

Stereotypes of the successful leader are still defined in today's world in masculine terms. For those who study stereotypes, there remain clear expectations for both male and female leaders in their stereotypical roles. And, both can suffer if they violate these expectations. We also have these same expectations specific to health and age. One's weight has a direct relationship with electability and one's "fitness" for office. People attach weight and health requirements with perceptions of "political leadership competence" (Bresnahan, et al., 2016).

Studies focused on weight and politics found that obese and overweight females who ran in 2008 and 2012 were eliminated during the primaries. Additionally, one study found that bigger males were favored while just the opposite was true for women.

The bigger, the better. Or, so they say. We associate leadership both with physical size and the physical structure of the face. One's bone structure, based on evolutionary studies, conclude that people prefer leaders with strong, dominant bone structures, like a pronounced jaw or chiseled features. Another stereotype suggests that taller people are more successful and that we assign them a prestigious status partially based on this factor.

We know that every president has an annual health exam and results are available for public review and comment. The mindset for most is that the person who leads this country should be healthy, strong, and have the stamina and discipline needed to lead. Most people think, *If you can't control yourself, then how will you be able to control the country? If you disregard your own health, then how will you treat the health of this country? If you are overweight, then are you going to have health issues and become sick?* Americans understand health and its implications.

In 2014, Hillary Clinton had a blood clot on the brain. The media questioned her fitness. Joe Biden had a series of brain aneurisms in the 1980s, and confidence in him wavered. President Trump's report of being in "perfect health" was questioned by many who challenged his reported weight by splashing unflattering photos of him across social media. News anchors worked hard to figure out his weight based on camera angles, and talk shows even interviewed doctors about Trump's annual exam findings.

The bottom line is that the issue of weight is stereotyped as bad, ugly, and negative. And, the media does a phenomenal job of reinforcing this. We see it with famous people who gain a pound or lose thirty. Unflattering "before and after" photographs are always making headlines. The subject of weight carries stigmas, including indifference, bad odor, laziness, looming sickness, and self-blame. The stigma against obesity is well-documented. From hiring practices, salary disparities, and promotion rates at work to social exclusion, fat jokes, and chubby-choice dating websites in personal settings—all in all, weight carries weight.

Age also has its labels and limitations. With the political spectrum ripe with candidates of all ages, there's a good chance that the media and voters will have much to say based on age, health, and the stamina for needed the position. We often try to guess someone's age in our heads by looking for nonverbal cues like wrinkles, age lines, glasses, neck skin, and conditions of the hands. A quick spring in the step lets us know that someone is healthy, when compared to a slower walk and smaller gait. In general, an older-looking appearance sparks questions about the overall physical, mental, and cognitive condition about someone.

You have to be thirty-five years old to run for the office of the president in America. Just by the very nature of that, age, like many other factors, plays a role in our politics. Age bias is discussed in the workplace, in relationships, and as a part of popular training programs focusing on the five generations currently in the workforce. As Kaufmann (2017) and others point out, older workers have negative stereotypes placed on them simply because of their real or perceived age. We are knowledgeable of age discrimination, but also question if older people should be hired for certain jobs. While there is evidence of competence as we age, negative stereotypes exist. Can an older adult handle the grueling schedule and tasks of the presidency?

In terms of crossing task-oriented expectations, an interesting outcome happened when men performed a traditionally female-oriented task. Men experienced increased self-consciousness, discomfort, and exhibited an increase in aggressiveness. The study found that men attempted to overcompensate for completing a woman's task merely based on its expected gender assignment.

We know that the type of task plays a role in how likely the person will emerge as a leader. For example, what if a female candidate pulled the door open for her male opponent to enter first? Or, what would happen if two males hugged rather than shake hands at the end of a heated conversation?

President Donald Trump and Indian Prime Minister Narendra Modi embrace while delivering joint statements in the Rose Garden of the White House on June 26, 2017.

We see a strikingly different image of President Trump embracing Indian Prime Minister Narendra Modi and this may challenge our stereotypical expectations of how male world leaders should physically behave.

Specifically, candidates must decide if task style and interpersonal style works for their campaigns. Task style refers to when the leader initiates and organizes work while laying out expectations and directions for how the work will be done. Or, interpersonal style in which the leader engages in activities to support the morale and welfare of people? As you can guess, masculine and feminine stereotypes also align with these styles and how leaders behave.

We also watch how leaders make decisions. Again, two basic styles are exhibited by those in power. Perhaps we are drawn to a candidate or leader who encourages followers to participate in making decisions. This democratic decision making tends to fall in line with the feminine stereotype due to its inclusion of others. Or, perhaps we are accepting of autocratic decision making? With this, the leader does not encourage participation, which is associated with the masculine stereotype of controlling others.

Regardless of task style or decision making preferences, stereotypical boost and stereotypical threat help us determine if our leaders are competent or not. Specifically, stereotypical boosting is the promotion of positive stereotypes, which leads to individuals being perceived as competent. Whereas stereotypical threat is the belief that negative stereotypes lead to individuals being perceived as less competent.

I advise that you always check yourself for your levels of bias and prejudice as you watch leaders emerge through a process of competition and elimination laden with labels and stereotypes. Watch the process of competition and elimination as candidates emerge to meet your in-group's needs. Will you demand agentic or communal traits? Will you know of candidates' childhood experiences that have molded them? Educate yourself beyond *E! News* and *People* magazine. Understand and defend how your candidate's party traits and labels align with your needs—and back it up with facts.

"Don't live up to your stereotypes."
—Sherman Alexie

CHAPTER 4

Our Emotional Connections: Understanding Our Emotional Biases and Biases in Politics

Emotion is defined as "an internal, mental state representing evaluative, balanced reactions to events, agents, or objects that vary in intensity . . . they are generally short-lived, intense, and directed at some external stimuli" (Hasell and Weeks, 2016). "Emotions are an important factor in how people respond" to different situations. Basically, they "stir people up" (Marcus, 2000).

Emotions are important for how we respond to people, situations, and challenges. While we like to think we use our brains to justify or reason, the truth is that our internal mental state is usually in control. Those two tiny, right and left lima bean-shaped amygdala nestled deep within our primitive limbic brain are partially responsible for how we have survived as human beings; today, they continue to drive how we feel, think, and act. We rely on our feelings, our gut instincts. In turn, our nonverbal actions are triggered. We all know what our basic, or core, emotions are and in terms of body language, we even know what they should look like on the outside.

People, like animals, shift their perceptions and goals, and redirect when suspicion arises. *Do I feel safe? Am I in trouble? What is wrong? Is someone lying to me?* On many occasions, certain behaviors spark our lie detection processes. When a person deviates from typical (or baseline) behaviors, we naturally seek out evidence to understand what is going on. In our brains, feelings of distrust and suspicion are activated by domain-specific mechanisms, including cognitive thoughts.

One's mood can be contagious. Political feelings are influential. Cognitive thought is a complex firing of rapid synapses, creating thought. Emotional appeals influence voting behaviors and alter how we engage and make choices. Campaigns flagrantly use visual imagery, music, and verbiage to evoke emotional responses from us.

Even the role of music and certain tones of voice elicit feelings from voters. Think of a candidate's theme song and how it made you feel. From "Don't Stop Believing" to "Celebrate" booming from a convention hall, thousands feel connected to their candidate as well as their fellow like-minded in-group peers.

While verbal content expresses ideas, nonverbals almost always express feelings. Albert Mehrabian's rule stands that seven percent of communication is verbal, thirty-eight percent is our tone of voice, and fifty-five percent comes from our body language. Collectively, these three elements transmit our messages. It's important to realize that more than half of how we communicate comes from our body language as part of nonverbal communication. Our nonverbal and emotional responses are quicker than cognitive thoughts and processed faster in our brains. Reasoning may be tossed aside in order to make room for a surge of emotions.

This is powerful in terms of advertising and social media. Eric Chemi and Nick Wells's (2015) online article, "Emotions, not facts, matter most in convincing voters" affirms that "[w]e can explain 90 percent of the change in voting intention by people's emotional response alone." Their *Copypop* study determined this by measuring only three advertising factors: how much people liked the ad, what emotion they felt, and how much they felt that emotion.

Many have studied emotions as they relate to current divergent political attitudes and see the influence of anger and anxiety in politics. Social media and other media outlets also know this and capitalize on it for ratings. When news coverage can evoke an emotional response, viewers are captivated to stay tuned or read more. Weeks (2016) pointed out that "fear (and anxiety) can be elicited through news media if there is perceived threat to an individual's personal safety or if the story lacks a causal factor for an event, which result in protective behaviors." It doesn't even have to be real—perception is enough for us.

Just the perception of something that engages us triggers emotional responses; in particular, fear and anxiety. They are important for self-preservation and protection. So, it makes sense that candidates talk incessantly about fear-based issues like the threat of nuclear war or North Korea's unstable leader while affirming their words with strong body and facial expressions. The notion that illegal immigrants will rape American women should make our blood boil.

We become emotionally invested when we see others suffer at the hands of immigration government officials. We stand ready to send troops abroad at the very thought of the "bad people" engaging in war with us. Whether or not any of these situations are true is somewhat irrelevant. It's the perception of it that triggers emotional responses. Fear is one of the most powerful and easy to understand emotions. Knowing this, two types of hierarchy come into play: dominance hierarchy and prestige hierarchy.

Dominance hierarchy status operates out of fear, intimidation, and consequences for failing to withdraw when challenged by the dominant person. These actions may be associated with settling disputes, including arguing and beating someone else.

Prestige hierarchy status is attained because people want to follow a high-status person. People are willing and even excited to follow their leader because they see the benefits that this person brings to their preferred groups and themselves. Studies suggest that this type of hierarchy evolved to help groups conform and even permit certain individuals to serve as role models and leaders within the group.

We are also emotionally invested and biased by stories about cheating, lying, and deception. Those are emotional triggers for us because we understand them on a personal level, not just a political level.

Putting it in plain terms, "the most effective messages related to emotions and relationships are nonverbal ones" (Demir, 2011). Especially with leadership groups who want their needs met. And usually based on what actions they see benefiting them.

We are visual beings. Seeing is our primary sense and the one our brains use to digest information. Visuals also generate emotions that are deeply rooted within our cortex at the limbic, or primitive, level. Visual coding is as old as human history. Prior to language constructs, visuals were used to communicate. This holds true today in that people give merit to what they see and the nonverbals that emanate from each of us.

What voters see is important in their decision-making process—both cognitively and emotionally. When information about a candidate is limited, we will fill in the blanks of our thought processes from visual images. YouTube videos, televised debates, and the incessant slew of campaign ads blaring through televisions are critical for connecting emotionally with candidates.

In political terms, the masses' mindset may examine a candidate to determine if his or her status falls within a dominant or prestige hierarchy in terms of how this person rose to power and how they will serve, lead, or rule the group. Understanding a person's social and political status helps a group understand the role of that person within the group. The group may clearly share their needs and challenges with the hope that their preferred leader will bring benefits and solutions to others.

Knowing that individuals favor their in-group systems and look at out-group members through negative lenses is key. For example, when a politician is a member of one's in-group, there are fewer negative judgments, according to some studies. This favoritism towards the people we like is obvious. Perhaps it goes back to the elementary school days of asking someone if they like you by checking "yes" or "no." Perhaps it's that simple and we grant passes to those we like. Bias comes in many formats, including in-group bias.

Styles vary, terms change, but the overall feelings that specific emotions solicit are noticed by people who, in turn, act or react.

Style	Values/Motivations	Descriptors
Agonic	Hedonic	Cultural interactions, behaviors
Agentic	Communal	Communication styles, stereotypes
Agency	Communion	Interpersonal styles

Diving deeper into the meaning of these terms and how they "look" to us is important since gender, stereotyping, and leadership roles are connected.

Style	Motivation	Communication Style	Behavior Perceptions	Focus	Gender
Agonic, Agentic, Agency	Self first	Compete and control	Strong, aggressive, confident, hard	Individual	Male
Hedonic, Communal, Communion	Others matter	Inclusive	Sensitive, kind, caring, emotional	People	Female

So, what happens when candidates violate these expectations of motivation, communication, and behavior? We react. Visually assertive gestures, being forceful, and being demanding hurt some candidates while others reap the benefits of taking charge. There are consequences for violating one's style, type, and gender. For example, when a male exhibits hedonic, communal, or communion-like behaviors, he is questioned as being "a real man" or called a whiney baby.

A crying man draws attention, and many question his strength or character because he broke from his gender-prescribed norms. For women, taking a hard-line position also solicits emotions and opinions from us. Some find her "difficult to work with" and, as we often hear, name-calling for being "tough" is rather unflattering.

I will say that times are changing, and biases are also shifting from traditional expectations. With round-the-clock access to media outlets, we have shifted from local to global. In turn, issues and norms are being challenged. For many, growth and change, though, remain emotionally draining or, at the least, emotional.

The media is relentless in tugging at our hearts and minds. By drawing us in, we are captivated and stay glued to one channel. In return, media outlets are rewarded via advertiser investments. So, it makes economic sense why outlets work hard to create and promote entertaining and captivating stories. An interesting point is the subject of the story. If it is about war or conflict, the anchors and interviewers typically scowl and are apt to use aggressive, challenging questions. On the flip side, a people-centric story holds our interest because we feel for the victim, the veteran, and family who, perhaps, just lost their home.

Remember the pass that America gifted Joe Biden when his son died of cancer. This human-interest story tamed the beasts so a father could mourn. Storylines temporarily shifted and images of father, son, and family consumed our visual landscape. But, now, front and center in politics, he's fair game once again.

Politicians' sentiments have a direct emotional effect on us. Facial expressions are powerful. As cameras hone in on candidates' faces, we assess the candidate and how she or he makes us feel. Watching their facial expressions and nonverbals gives us extra insight as to the character of a person. In turn, their actions either validate or violate their words—and we are sensitive to that.

We learn best by seeing these images in our brain, both cognitively and emotionally. Science has proven that our eyes send data to our nervous system quicker than any other sense. This rapid fire process is key for preserving ourselves as well as for processing information from our environment. So, it makes sense that seeing candidates and watching them speak and act carries a lot of weight.

Given the chance to listen to a politician or watch him or her, the vast majority of people will opt to watch. We remember images that we see much more than what we hear. Findings also suggest that this is true for images that elicit disgust, fear, and anger. Those particular emotions make people want to act or react; meaning, individuals may feel compelled to do something. For example, after 9/11, military enlistment rates spiked because people felt compelled to act.

During the 2000 presidential election between George W. Bush and Al Gore, studies found that the use of images on particular social media sites elicited feelings of warmth and likeability to garnish popularity. Verner and Wicks's (2006) research of Bush and Gore concluded that Gore used more images surrounding himself with regular people as a way to connect with regular people. Viewers were drawn to his "he's just like me" persona.

Al Gore laughs during an appearance at Medgar Evers College in Brooklyn.

Goodnow (2013) found that Obama's and Romney's campaigns used Facebook to appeal to viewers and this left an image for voters. We connect with leaders when they display appropriate nonverbal emotions. This leadership performance is just that: a performance. Candidates would be well served to master their roles.

Interpersonal nonverbal cues strike emotional responses from our brains. Nonverbal mirroring in our brains stimulates us emotionally. The current political landscape includes both men and women, candidates of color, varying sexual orientations, and different faiths.

To help voters emotionally connect to a particular subject, strategists will pair vivid, threatening images to specific statements because watching something makes us feel something. When we are tuned into a TV show or visual image on our cell phones, our attitudes are being shaped by what we see. Watch a news story in which the anchor is talking while a video is silently playing in the background. We hear the words of the journalist, but we are drawn to what is happening in the image. These often close-up displays are intentionally concocted to make us feel a particular emotion. Again, this is intentional. Give this a try: turn the sound off while watching TV; odds are you can follow along just by watching the people on the screen. Emotions pop and nonverbals captivate us.

But what is that emotion? Media editing plays a large role in showing us only what they want us to see. As a result of this, we may feel angry, sad, or compelled to act or at least comment on what we see at that moment. Often, these visual clips are taken out of reference, and the viewer fails to find out the entire story. Yet our reactions and our feelings stick with us.

Emotional expression by political leaders has a direct effect on TV viewers, including both positive and negative feelings about the person being viewed. We are able to make an emotional connection with a candidate or leader simply by watching him or her on television. We are drawn to baby faces, including President Bush with his childlike face. We like Vice President Gore's chiseled face with strong jawline that oozes confidence and draws us to him. You know, he just has "that" look. Believe me, "that" look is clearly rooted in science and human behavior.

Journalists, news anchors, and notable experts' personal views towards political figures cause bias between the candidate and the viewer at home. We are impacted by how the politician is interviewed or described by the news anchor. There is a link between visual bias and voter opinion. Negative action shots are used more by the media against political figures. Use of advertising and certain emotions lead to either feelings of enthusiasm or fear/anxiety depending on the ad. Anger is the most potent emotion.

Lindsey Graham shouts while questioning Judge Brett Kavanaugh during his Supreme Court confirmation hearing.

For example, Senator Lindsey Graham's anger is obvious as he defends Judge Brett Kavanaugh during Kavanaugh's Supreme Court confirmation hearing on September 27, 2018. Graham's facial expressions, hand gestures, and body movements clearly convey his anger.

Psychologically and emotionally, we want to make sense of someone's behaviors. Research says that when people are successful, they attribute this to personal factors; yet when they fail, external reasons are used to rationalize the outcomes; somebody or some condition is blamed. This self-serving mindset works well when things go our way and our candidate wins. But we struggle when we fail to get what we want. The blame game commences.

Today's information-saturated environment impacts what we think and feel. People express their views on social media, respond to others' online posts and blogs, and feel compelled to make themselves heard. As a result, emotions are heightened, and many are on edge. This ultra-sensitive environment we are in makes almost everyone anxious.

From watching road rage unfold before us on TV to reading about the latest racial atrocity online, we are hot and ready to respond. Facebook, Twitter, and Instagram are free, easy-to-use online platforms in which Americans seek their news, express their political views, and respond to others who either share or challenge their viewpoints.

Recent literature suggests that partisan news sources, social media, and our emotional responses are linked. By posting stories and photographs that spark anger and anxiety, people are influenced and react. Toss on the political piece, and the scene is ideal for emotions to run high and people to feel intensely.

Negative news is stronger and longer lasting than positive news. Think about what you remember from your past. Where were you on 9/11? How about when Kennedy was shot? And, what about the twenty children slaughtered at Sandy Hook? It's fairly easy to recall, in detail, events which traumatize you. The same goes for news stories; the more tragic, the more memorable. And, this is constantly reinforced by the news.

When the news reports on current events like crime, war, and human survival stories, we empathize with those who are affected. The news knows this—they even warn us of what we are about to see on the air. Yet we still watch. The vivid image of Salvadoran migrant Oscar Martinez Ramirez and his daughter consumed our news programs and online accounts. Both drowned while trying to cross the Rio Grande on their way to the US on June 24, 2019, becoming the poster family for illegal immigration fiercely debated during numerous 2020 presidential debates.

Watch the debates and, for every issue presented, candidates share personal stories to hook us and make us emotionally connect with them.

- "My grandparents immigrated to this country . . . "
- "My dad was a veteran . . ."
- "My daughter battled childhood cancer. . .."
- "When I served in our nation's military and completed three overseas deployments . . ."
- "My sister is a single mother without insurance . . ."

When news coverage angers people or covers conflict without solutions, this threatens us and who we are. It challenges our democracy and feelings of control and choice. Stories and dramatization are an effort to capture our attention. And, of course, negative, scary, fear-based, and emotional news sells. By watching people suffer, we empathize with them, and they become relatable. With just one misstep, we could be them. And that, my ready-to-vote readers, scares us into paralysis, apathy, or action.

One study looked at leader sympathy characteristics, which included trustworthiness, inspiration, knowledge, awareness of common people's opinions and thoughts, sincerity, qualifications, good leadership, personal charisma, and consistency. Drawing again on the fact that gender evokes an emotional response from us, these sympathetic behaviors impact how we feel and how we pick a certain candidate. We are also able to see these characteristics through body language like smiling, eye contact, leaning in, and welcoming hand gestures.

For survival reasons deeply rooted within genetics, we associate physical strength with leadership strength. Individuals with dominant and pronounced facial lines and larger body structures are preferred. Work on physical formidability in human social status confirms that perceptions of strength and leadership are connected. So, if we assign physical size with social rank, then logic says that the perceived 'bigger' person will win the presidency. The candidate who looks big to us, in many ways like size, self-control, and ability to make big gains for our country, not only makes sense to our brain, but touches us emotionally. The media even reinforces this by positioning the cameras on-stage at such angles which make the candidates appear bigger.

While ideas are usually expressed through the spoken work, feelings tend to be expressed through nonverbals. Campaign strategists know this and capitalize on it. For example, touch sears feelings into our psyches. For some, this may create an everlasting feeling of warmth. For others, a burning pain sensation. It depends on numerous nonverbal cues acting simultaneously. Haptics, the science of stimulating the sense of touch, is involved in nonverbal communication and how our bodies physically interact.

Rep. Tim Ryan, Sen. Cory Booker, New York City Mayor Bill De Blasio, former housing secretary Julian Castro and Sen. Elizabeth Warren embrace after the first night of the Democratic presidential debate on June 26, 2019.

Physical conditions also alter other body parts, including our eyes—the windows to our soul. A shift in our blink rates can also be tied to our emotions in that when we feel something, usually fear or anxiety, our blink rates change. Of course, other conditions like lighting, temperature, humidity, allergies, screen time, reading, weariness, and mental loads also cause our eyes to "talk." Our peepers have a language all their own and we should closely watch.

Experts have found that tasks involving memory and heavier cognitive load, meaning that we have to think about something, tend to increase blink rates, whereas concentration activities like studying and reading tend to decrease blinking. We do know that emotions and blinking are connected, and with anger and excitement, blinking significantly increases. Some studies suggest that anxiety and frustration cause blink rates to shift from baseline (normal) rates. When Nixon was pelted with questions about the Watergate scandal, his blink rate increased and did not go unchecked by strategists to confirm his anxiety with the situation.

Bucy (2016) and others' extensive research connecting emotions to blink rates yielded notable results.

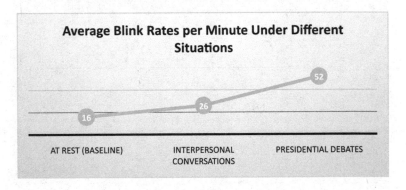

During the January 2012 Republican presidential debate, researchers conducted blink rate studies and found that candidate Rick Santorum "out-blinked the entire field of GOP contenders" with sixty-one blinks per minute. Romney averaged thirty-four blinks per minute and the remainder of the candidates averaged twenty-eight blinks per minute. No doubt, Santorum was emotionally charged.

Of course, we expect blink rates to increase under stressful conditions like debates and intense conversations, but when a significantly higher blink rate is noticed, other factors like heightened anxiety, heavy cognitive (thought) load, and preoccupation might be at play. Other factors include high stress environments like an auditorium stage with hot lights, multiple cameras, and ramped up audience members ready to pounce.

During the 2004 presidential debates, George W. Bush's increased blink rates signaled that his stress levels were elevated. With insurmountable evidence of cognitive strain, heightened stress levels, and increased blinking, one can almost see a candidate struggle or even unravel under these conditions. Bring in nonverbals and external factors and the scene is set to go well or crash in today's high stakes, highly contested political platforms.

Ekman's (2009) extensive work with emotions and detecting deception provides us with a wealth of nonverbal, tonal cues, and body behaviors for which we can see, hear, process, and judge. These actions, and how we react, are directly tied to our emotions. As we watch candidates perform on stage and engage with potential voters to win them over, we intentionally should look for some of the following behavioral clues and what they might actually mean. Remember, these powerful nonverbals carry more weight than words, especially when the two systems of communication do not align. When this is the case, we will default to the body language.

What we see	What it means
Facial micro expression, quick squelched expression	Triggering an emotion (distress, surprise, shock, disagreement)
Looking away, blushing, facial reddening	Embarrassment
Change in breathing, swallowing, increased blinking, sweating	Arousal of an emotion, a change in the baseline behavior

Facial blanching, blotchiness	Fear, anger
Jaw clenching	Frustration, anger
Lips pursed together	Holding back words
Change in breathing, chest movement	Nervous, anxious, calming self

The same applies to what we hear in terms of speech or tone of voice. Specifically:

What we hear	**What it means**
Speech errors, pausing	Not prepared, unsure, caught off guard, nervous
Faster speech, raised pitch, skin reddening, louder, speech errors	Fear, anxiety, anger
Pitch raised or lowered	Negative emotion: anger, sadness, fear

Clifford's (2019) work on how our emotions frame moral issues and polarize us found that our emotions do, indeed, impact how we frame issues. Clifford also found that our emotions influence public opinion.

When we belong to a group, we assign our emotions to align with our group. The "we" concept enables us to show support with others who share our thoughts and feelings about a particular issue or candidate. Research confirms that in-group membership leads to more positive thoughts about the in-group's choice and more negative bias towards the competitors. So, when we like someone, we think good thoughts about them and even dismiss their naughty behaviors. Remember Ronald Reagan's Iran-Contra Affair? Richard Nixon's Watergate? Bill Clinton's inappropriate relationship?

Even when moral issues fire us up, parties and their faithful followers will go to their respective corners to defend their candidates on their choices of polarized issues like the death penalty and stem cell research. Issues like these elicit strong emotions from us and we are usually unwilling to compromise. We also will not tolerate those who disagree with us, digging in even when our emotions come up against moral dilemmas or ethical challenges.

Clifford (2019) noted that a recent "longitudinal study found that feelings of hostility, but not fear or beliefs about harm, predicted increases in moral conviction in the context of an election." That is powerful for gathering votes and swaying people to a candidate's side; as long as we can be morally aligned, we are then a part of a particular camp. Latner (2013) even suggests that love, pride, guilt, shame, and envy are emotional triggers of attraction.

Sadness and anxiety appear to not be linked to moral issues; therefore, our emotions and reactions are quite different than disgust and anger, which can compel us to act or act out.

Disgust and anger, however, are two emotions which we understand without much convincing. Disgust is associated with terms like impurity, tainted, aversion, distaste, abhorrence, and loathing. It is actually the primary physical/behavioral action for physical distance or avoidance. Disgust is an important emotion for keeping us away from something harmful. Evidence provides a link between disgust and morality by condemning those who do not confirm with our views and we are justified by moral righteousness. Clifford's 2019 work on feelings of internal disgust are associated with moral judgments and violations. Actions rooted in disgust tend to look like social exclusion and gossip.

For example, National Security Advisor John Bolton may only have been listening to the May 2018 conversation between President Trump and Secretary General of the North Atlantic Treaty Organization (NATO), but he sure was thinking something—it's all over his face and, it's not encouraging (below). Many facial expressions that we display are quickly identifiable; in particular, we are sensitive to negative and warning nonverbals.

Think about anger and how someone looks when he or she is angry. It's obvious. It's rooted in the behavioral expectation that, when an event is negative, someone is responsible for its negative impact. When we feel anger, we are usually annoyed, irritated, resentful, and/or displeased. The literature on anger states that anger is used to handle social rule violations. We become angry when unfair actions come our way and we must react. Research continues to stress that anger is linked to aggression and action.

Anger makes people get involved. It's actually one of the only emotions which prompts people to act. The Trump campaign knows this and has even incorporated it into campaign rallies. President Trump rewards the crowd for getting unruly; he all but says that it's acceptable for people to act on their anger, which elicits fear in many. Anger also increases information sharing as we seek out like-minded angry people. The sheep or mob mentality might be at play. Injustice, or the perception of it, elicits feelings of anger or rage, whereas cooperation lends itself to allies and harmony.

It makes sense that positive moods and behaviors produce more positive judgments, while negative moods and behaviors create more negative judgments. The literature states that emotions serve to evaluate situations and our place in them, by proxy or in actuality. We reward cooperation and punish noncooperation, even if no gains will be made by punishment. Our emotional need for cooperation is strong. We want people to get along.

Anxiousness or anxiety is another influential emotion and fairly easy to see through body language. When feeling anxiety, people want to engage in activities that reduce the emotional and physical symptoms that go with anxiety. Anxiety, along with anger, motivates people to take an interest in politics. When people take an interest, control is then gained and both anxiety and anger can be better managed.

Anxiety is considered negative and people want to avoid it. On the other end, enthusiasm is a positive trait and we are attracted to it. We can be altruistic when we believe we will not be harmed. Anxiety and fear are reactive threats and make people break from the norm, their routines. Without fear of a threat, predictable, calm behaviors are expected and governed by a sense of routine. When politicians use enthusiasm and fear, responses are almost guaranteed. Specifically, being enthusiastic motivates us to engage and remain loyal; triggering fear "stimulates vigilance" and facilitates persuasion. Successful campaigns appeal to our emotions to obtain desirable outcomes and actions rooted in predictable emotions and behaviors. Remember, President Obama gave Americans "Hope."

Emotions help us understand why some people act differently or break from their normal behaviors. They might be "acting out of character" in a situation. We attach emotion to a candidate and how she or he will make decisions as we watch the interplay of thought and feeling. Weeks (2016) suggest that partisan news followers are the most politically engaged and have a lot of knowledge compared to ill-informed citizens. Few argue the partisan slants of Fox News and MSNBC.

Marcus's (2000) work on emotions in the political sector found that we assign emotions to "external events, symbols, situations, individuals, or groups, in order to provoke a reaction in the audience." When we take a lot of time to think about an issue, we give pause to our emotions by slowing their natural desire to react quickly. However, when savvy political campaigns get us to feel something based on what we see, we quickly react.

Candidates must be cautious so as not to let their negative memories or emotions drive their political beliefs. As people, we are influenced by our pasts, which drive our futures. This emotional bias can either work in a candidate's favor or haunt them.

Empathy is considered altruistic and we are drawn to those who appear to care for us. The emotional empathic response is important for initiating the perception of a helping behavior. It bonds us with another.

Our emotional responses stem from judgments stored in our memories or in reaction to an event or situation that triggers us. One expert points out that emotional responses can also be "hedonic" or "agnostic." Morality, of course, is interlaced with our emotional justifications.

Hedonic emotions touch on a person's pleasure or points of pain specific to their willingness to move towards something positive or away from something threatening. This is based on the belief that people will avoid pain and seek pleasure. Applying this to candidates' motives, they aim to help followers feel welcome and feel that what they promote will create a pleasurable experience.

On the other end of emotional responses, **agnostic emotions** elicit more doubtful or skeptical responses. These negative emotions make us question candidates as well as ourselves. It is not a condition in which people want to stay. We cannot stand uncertainty and will not tolerate it from our leaders. Scandals and rumors will kick into high gear. We know these sentiments well; the media and gossip-based syndicates bank on it.

Our emotional reactions to a leader's race, age, and social class are additional attributes that guide our emotional compasses.

Controlling one's emotions is critical for public office; command of one's body is imperative. With the art of negotiation, one's display of emotion is expected to be "neither too intense nor too controlled" (Eagly and Heilman, 2016).

Further, we are drawn to confidence and the emotions it evokes in us for how we expect our leader to behave. Confidence is infectious and those seeking it will be drawn to those who demonstrate it. Everyone wants to be seen with a winner.

I recommend that you, the sage voter, not assume or assign a particular style or label to the candidates until you first educate yourself through direct viewing without political commentary. Watch and identify those emotions. Stop knee-jerk reactions and buying into social media heart tugs. Fight the urge to pick an agentic leader over a communal one—even though we feel drawn to the agentic style. Suspend candidate and voting judgments until you have control of your own emotions and can vote with cognitive and emotional clarity. Knowledge is power.

"The road to victory is paved with emotional intentions."
—Drew Westen

CHAPTER 5

Liar, Liar, Politician's on Fire: Spotting Deception Not Often Noticed as We Watch Leaders

√   Sweating
√   Flushing
√   Blanching
√   Wringing the hands
√   Picking at the fingernails
√   Rubbing hands together
√   Tone of voice
√   Vibrations in the voice
√   Stuttering

People have observable body movements and nonverbal cues when lying. While the list I just provided is not exhaustive, there are signs that infer deception. But there is no one, single nonverbal that serves as proof of lying. It's harder to discern than that. And, remember, a good liar knows this list, is well-rehearsed, and banks on how his or her audience will respond.

"People are poor lie detectors. This isn't the kind of task we're naturally good at. There are clues that humans do naturally when they are being deceptive, but we're not paying close enough attention to pick them up. We're not counting how many times a person says 'I' or looks up. We're focusing on a higher level of communication" (Mihalcea, 2015).

We don't like liars. But everyone lies. It is a skill for surviving that we, as animals, have learned in order to navigate our world and survive in social situations. While some people fib now and then, there are those who lie and deceive so often that we continue to wonder where truth stops and lying begins. And, for most of us, we understand and accept the fact that our political leaders lie as well. It comes with the job.

We are hardwired for deception and neuroscientists note that spontaneous lying activates a different part of the brain versus telling planned or rehearsed lies. Think about the load on the cognitive structures of our brains needed to hold and promote a lie. The body, the words, and the brain must work in sync to deliver and sustain the deception or lie.

Many study lying and deception, and the verbal and nonverbal cues associated with these behaviors. From body leaks to emotional displays, lying and deception are complex issues to study. Rarely are concrete answers provided.

In our heads, we lie for a few reasons. Sometimes we need to protect ourselves. For example, someone might deny spreading a rumor or gossiping because it's not morally or ethically right to do that. No one likes to be called out for those behaviors. Others lie to steer clear of conflict or tension in social situations. Imagine a party and you don't like one of the people attending; yet, you smile and engage with them as though everything is grand. When, in reality, you'd like to run away or tell the person to leave you alone. These tend to be called low-stake lies in that the risk for telling it and the outcomes for getting caught are low. Also, the receiver of the fib is unlikely to challenge it. We know this and have a lot of practice with it. "I'm good." "Nothing's wrong." "No problem." "We're on the same page." "It's fine." You know these statements.

Another reason we lie is to avoid hurting others' feelings. I have heard a few people gloss over the truth when asked, "How do I look?" or "What do you think?" Sometimes it's just easier to slide ever so slightly off the truth wagon in order to preserve the situation.

Keeping these reasons in mind, think about how and why politicians lie. Perhaps they've been accused of something. Or, they said something that contradicted something they said previously.

So, how do we become better at catching deception from our politicians? Many will not take the time to figure it out. Choosing to not investigate all of the evidence is okay for some people. It's too time-consuming—and having access to all of the facts is highly unlikely. So, why bother? Let someone else do the investigating.

Some people are just good at lying. Others not so much. The best ones are able to disarm suspicion, control their emotions, display attractive nonverbals, and know the psychology of people and behaviors. They mirror others, use engaging posture, shift in the right direction, gesture, nod, look, smile, and speak in such ways that they appear believable. Some liars should receive awards for their performances because they are just plain believable. They have rehearsed for hours and actually look forward to their show. For some, it's a game and they want to win.

Sometimes it's also easier to just let it go. We want to invest our time where we get the greatest return. And, getting proof of a lie may require a lot of time. We rationalize this in our own minds first. While lying has a subtle and fairly dependable set of rules in that liars tend to provide fewer details and less plausible answers, this is not significant enough for us to become Nancy Drew or Sherlock Holmes.

A good liar knows the basics of how to spot deception—the failure to make eye contact, sweating, pursing of the lips, and other nonverbal behaviors that the average person picks up on quickly.

A liar's countermeasures include lots of eye contact and smiling while displaying behaviors that make him or her look credible. One communication rule says that we look at each other while speaking. So, a liar would know this as well and look right at you while spewing dishonesties. And a good politician knows that fearful people show more startled responses.

Let's think about this and how most of us view lying. We might feel guilty and fear getting caught. This is not the case for everyone. And, in politics, there is a baseline expectation that politicians lie and it's a part of the job. This rhetoric is sad, but true. They also get a lot of practice telling lies. This might be important in that they are able to "test" their lies and tweak their words and behaviors for the next show. A good actor always seeks to improve their performance.

US President Donald Trump speaks to the media as he departs the White House.

Of course, we must be cautious as to not jump to conclusions with the first signs of deception. It is not that simple. Researchers have labeled this the "Othello error" based on the Shakespearean character. Othello accused his wife of infidelity, and his wife was notably upset. Othello misinterpreted this behavior as proof of her cheating and had her "suspected" lover killed. The sense of urgency caused Othello to have tunnel vision, as he failed to consider any cues of truthfulness from his wife. In the end, he killed his wife, as well. Such a tragedy, but then again, it's Shakespeare.

We voters must be cautious as to not do the same as we attempt to make sense of the political arena and high stakes of selecting a president. Do we discount truthfulness cues and see crying as weakness or yelling as anger? Is a hand covered mouth a cue to deception, as displayed during a 2013 Senate hearing on sexual assaults in the military?

Chief of Staff of the Air Force Gen. Mark Welsh III testifies with U.S. military leaders before the Senate Armed Services Committee on pending legislation regarding sexual assaults in the military June 4, 2013 in Washington, DC.

This is difficult detective work, even for the most skilled lie detection expert. The rules that we as a society have agreed to play by do not fit into a savvy liar's schema. One of the toughest decisions a deceiver has to make is how to craft and edit the lie. The liar must decide which rules to adhere to and which to twist. Let's examine some of the rules as part of the deception process so that you may be alert for when it happens.

Anchoring

Salespeople are masters at starting at a price and then subtly manipulating their words and actions to make it appear that the first price (anchor) and the outcome (final price) are naturally aligned. Some call this "bait and switch," in that what you bargained for and thought you were getting were not the same at the end. It's a savvy tactic. A politician may anchor a story with lots of details in truth, but then switch it up with subtle lies. We basically don't hear the lie, or the liar makes it fit with the story—so we dismiss our first concern. As listeners, we nod in agreement with the truths being told and when a little lie is interjected, our brains and short-term memories let it slide, since it doesn't fit in our constructs. We are preoccupied and satisfied.

Truth-bias

Think about relationships. Trust and truth serve as the pillars for strong relationships. We watch a trusted person's body language and are constantly reaffirmed that their actions are truthful. We notice their facial expressions and are constantly assured as these facial cues display truthfulness. These are quick judgments and happen without much thought. Research on trustworthiness states that we know whether or not to trust someone or something in a third of a second. A split second is enough confirmation for us. And, as I mentioned previously, we grant passes to those we favor. So, heck, what's the harm in stretching the truth or accepting a little untruth?

Probing

After we ask a few clarifying questions when we have doubts about the truthfulness of something, we want to be satisfied with the details that were provided by us. We want to believe. It's in most of our natures, especially for those we trust or choose to follow. Politically speaking, we select a candidate because their answers, after media probing, satisfy us. We also believe their body language—nodding heads, lots of eye contact, and outstretched hands. People will come to the defense of their politicians whom they have never actually even met. It's loyalty by proxy. And, we do not like when the media hounds our favorites.

Facial appearance

Yes, we judge people based on how their faces look and what emotions are expressed through them. Those with attractive, symmetrical, or baby faces appear honest. Those with asymmetrical or odd looking characteristics can elicit anger or unkindness, and even dishonesty based on research findings. One interesting study theorized that there are faces that look "criminal." Do we have candidates or politicians with political looking faces? We hear people say that "he looks presidential" and I encourage you to figure out what that actually means. As a part of facial appearance, Ekman (2009) spent decades looking at micro expressions. These are defined as "full-face emotional expressions that are compressed in time, lasting only a fraction of their usual duration, so quick they are usually not seen."

Visual cue primacy

This rule suggests that we apply our visual detective skills in an attempt to detect a liar or deceptive behavior. It goes with the mantra of "seeing is believing." If we saw it, then it must be true. Situational factors influence how we process visual and nonverbal cues. We then determine what's important and what isn't, primarily based on visuals. And so we forget anything rational, and just go with what we see because "seeing is believing." Not so quick, Detective.

Single cue rule

This simply states that all liars, in any condition, can be stopped with clear-cut clues. For example, look away and you are lying; look at me and you are telling the truth. This, as we know, has been debunked in numerous studies. A pathological liar will stare right at you while telling you the moon is made of cheese. A deviant politician will stare at the camera while feeding the public a pile of deceptive garbage. Blink. Blink. Blink. Smile. Smile. Smile. Nod. Nod. Nod.

We must be careful that we do not fall into any of these traps as we seek answers from our leaders. A word of caution should be included in that nonverbals, gestures, words, and behaviors are culturally based. In America, we look at the other person as a sign of respect; whereas in many Asian and Latin countries, looking down indicates respect. We must be sensitive to our global environment and how it influences our thoughts and decisions. Educate yourself on these differences.

So, what do we do to detect deception and understand the dynamics specific to liars and lying? Studies suggest that we must look deeper into nonverbals. A shift of the eyes or quick swallow cannot and should not be the only indicators of falsities. It is much more intricate than that. It is the culmination of watching, listening, and repetition that will help us detect deception.

While we may literally hear everything going around us as part of a primitive survival activity, we should perhaps focus on the elements of the voice as a way to catch a liar. Vocal cues may provide the answers needed. Couple this with watching a suspect's nonverbals and a different picture may begin to form. For example, below is a picture of President Trump's former lawyer, Michael Cohen's testimony before the House Oversight Committee in 2019. He was found guilty of making false statements, including lying to Congress. I suggest you find this taped event and watch it as a learning opportunity. Cohen did an excellent job of letting his nonverbals lead.

Michael Cohen, former attorney and fixer for President Donald Trump, testifies before the House Oversight Committee on Capitol Hill February 27, 2019 in Washington, DC.

Tone

Below are seven tonal and style elements. Some are a part of our physical structure and some are able to be controlled by the person. By learning this nonverbal aspect of communication (about thirty-eight percent of communication, as will be discussed in the next chapter), you will become a more discreet viewer, judge, and voter.

1. **Amplitude**: Yell at me and I hear you; I'm not happy, but you have my attention. Often, the louder someone gets, the less she or he feels heard. So, screaming may be one way to understand the emotions of someone who is yelling at us from the screen. We have a preferred volume and when people violate it by whispering or roaring, we take notice. How loud is your favorite candidate? Whose voice commands the stage during a debate because it's the

loudest? And, do we even hear their words or are we just entertained?

2. **Pitch**: Often, I hear pitch elevate and think, *Defensive! What did I trigger in that person?* The pitch of the voice is connected to emotions and, when deception enters the scene, the pitch changes and tends to become elevated. I have heard many people who are attempting to lie use a higher pitch in order to convince me that they are being truthful. I'm not buying it. I hear the change in tone—most of us do. We are also attracted to people with lower pitched voices. Research suggests that males in their forties and fifties have more alluring pitches than with men in their thirties, or sixties and seventies.

3. **Resonance**: Morgan Freeman's voice of God is more believable due to his deep voice. Audiences like it. We also are attracted to certain radio or podcast personalities because of the powerful and lasting effect it has on us. Politically speaking, we like the deep, full, and reverberating voice of a leader in charge. We also believe this tone of voice because it's absent of squeakiness and high-pitch defensiveness. So, what does this mean for a female politician?

4. **Quality**: A quality voice commands attention, gets interrupted less, sounds "truthful," and is assigned to a high status leader. This voice evokes distinct emotional reactions from us. We question its authenticity when our leader's words do not match his or her voice quality or body language. We question why they are faltering, and why their breathing seems off. Might they be lying?

5. **Speech Rate**: Talk too much and you might be lying. Clam up and we question if you are hiding something. There's a fine balance between the two because people talk at trackable speech rates, measured in words per

minute. When we see the mouth moving "a mile a minute," we think and see an uncontrolled person—not an attractive quality. But say very little and you might be accused of "clamming up" to cover up.

6. **Latency Time**: You know this one . . . it's when someone mows right over you when you are speaking, or when it takes them "forever" to respond. When the babbler can't come up for air, we think, *Is he trying to cover his butt?* Or, *Why is she oversharing?* Or, there is silence after a question is posed. Crickets. We quickly wonder why this person won't respond. Perhaps staying quiet is better than uttering a lie. Whichever the case, this wait time between people speaking piques our interest if the nonverbal expectation is violated.

7. **Freudian slips**: Oops, a lie just fell out of that politician's mouth and we caught it. In actuality, this unintentional error in speech, memory, or physical action reveals something in their subconscious, and often true, feelings. But are these actual lies? These political gaffes add to a candidate's reputation and are often the source of late night comedic reactions. A few notable examples:

» Senator Ted Kennedy: "The breast and the brightest."
» Secretary of State Hillary Clinton: "First time home boners."
» Chicago Mayor Richard Daley, Sr.: "A policeman is there to preserve disorder."
» Vice President Joe Biden: "Start to see unemployment grow this spring."
» President George H. W. Bush: "We've had some sexbacks."
» President George W. Bush: "I think the world would be better off if we did leave."

We need to listen and watch what a candidate is saying and doing for the subtle, or even not so subtle, elements of his or her voice; at the same time, we must always watch his or her movements and gestures.

If you think about it, this is a full body activity for the liar, and it takes a lot of concentration to pull off. From the rehearsed words to the intentional gestures, coupled with the "right" tone, these layers of action take effort and are hard to sustain for long periods of time. Studies recommend that we pay attention by implementing three steps:

1. **Establish** a candidate's baseline nonverbals and then apply these to what is being said. Meaning, watch for how he or she normally behaves and speaks under no-stress conditions. Listen to the tone and watch how he or she postures the body and displays facial expressions.

2. **Watch** both the verbal and the nonverbals but try to not connect the two; this might be hard. Record candidate interviews, speeches, and debates. Watch and watch again. Learn.

3. **Listen** to the content of what is being said and watch for nonverbal behaviors that either support or challenge the words. Small cues may emerge and change when the deceptive candidate is saying truthful statements versus shifting into deceptive mode. For example, if good news is being uttered and then detailed, nonverbals should lean towards positive motions like small head nods or genuine smiles while engaging with the whole audience. Deceptive cues, on the other hand, could include sealing the lips tightly together, a change in blink rate, or small self-soothing gestures like one hand holding the other.

A lot of research has been linked to lying/deception and blink rates. Extensively studied, the number of times we blink is noticed by viewers. However, when conditions change, so do our blink rates.

While there are medical conditions linked to blinking, emotional shifts can also cause this nonverbal to react. The eye blink is a reflex in which the orbicularis muscles contract in response to a stimulus. This is part of our body's defense mechanism.

This combination of pictures shows US Speaker of the House Nancy Pelosi (D-CA)(L) talking about health-care legislation on Capitol Hill, March 26, 2019, in Washington, DC. US President Donald Trump announces a new immigration proposal, in the Rose Garden of the White House in Washington, DC, on May 16, 2019.

A combination of body actions and verbal statements should share and feed off of each other. While a politician may be excited to talk about a new trade deal and its success, the rise and fall of the chest in rapid movements exudes excitement. Quick air intakes are more indicative of panic or anxiety, not excitement. And, a change in skin color or sweating most likely negates authentic excitement and successful verbiage.

A part of the deception process is the fact that the liar must think about actions and words, while constantly adjusting to ensure that he or she is not caught. This requires a lot of work on the brain. Specifically, the liar must simultaneously think, act, and react while mentally staying steps ahead of what will happen next. That's taxing on one's cognitive processes. Liars are in a constant state of preparing what to say. This is planned and thought out. Truth tellers, when questioned as part of one study, focused on telling the story and what happened compared to the liars' use of fewer details. It's easier to tell the truth because it always stays the same.

Denial is a formidable approach for a liar who does not want to get caught. Guilty parties tend to use avoidance tactics by keeping the details fuzzy or attempting to confuse the listener. The opposite can be said about a truth teller. She or he is eager to come forth with details and repeat these as often as necessary, because that is the way it happened. Liars have to keep their deceptive ducks in a row at all times.

Examining body language, liars tend to present fewer torso movements and decreased hand and arm movements; overall, liars exhibit less limb movement. Additionally, we see an increase in eye and eyebrow movement—they typically look around more. Even with supportive evidence, we maintain our views and may be hesitant to call out someone as a liar. It's a strong accusation and we don't want to be wrong.

Lying is more stressful than telling the truth because of the difficulty of task, the guilt associated with deception, the fear of being found out, or knowledge kept secret. The body wants to ooze the truth. In some situations, liars use fewer illustrative hand movements and speak in higher pitched voices. Studies found that the higher pitched voice was more nervous and less fluent. Observers flagged less fluent, less serious, less empathic, and more nervous answers as lies. I challenge you to think about this as you watch and listen to both male and female candidates.

As we look for truths, we draw upon 1. verbal content cues; 2. auditory and paralinguistic cues; and 3. visual cues. Specifically, a long list of characteristics for determining deception include:

- Verbal cues that are consistent between answers and knowledge. Enough detail is provided by the candidates verbally that it is socially acceptable.
- Concreteness in which the candidate's answer is filled with details around the facts.

- Priori plausibility, meaning that a person's answer seems like a "likely" response for the person saying it. For example, a baker not knowing the difference between baking soda and baking powder would not seem plausible; whereas, a baker's knowledge of types of dough recipes seems plausible.

- Consistent answers are a clue for determining if what a candidate said earlier in a conversation aligns with a current answer. Or, did he or she contradict themselves?

- Auditory and paralinguistic markers for pitch, loudness, length of an answer, fluidity of speech, and wait time before answering a question.

- Visual cues triggering observer interest include smiling, gaze avoidance, shifting one's body, self-touch or manipulation, limb movement of the upper and lower body, showing the tongue, and drawing or hiding the lips.

- Talk time, similar to verbal cues, is also a recognizable nonverbal in that people know how long someone consumes a dialogue or air space. News anchors often comment on the length of time someone talks or if they respond with "no comment."

- Filling the unspoken space with "well, um, ah," and the like are indicators that deviate from a candidate's answer and are easily picked up by a voter.

- When listeners hear or see stuttering, broken phrases, or other speech errors, they are apt to raise a mental red flag.

- The time a person spends smiling is yet another cue and clue to what's really going on nonverbally. Too quick and it might be insincere. Too long and it seems forced.

- Movements of the body also can indicate deception or truth. When we see self-soothing behaviors like scratching, smoothing, or stroking of the body, the candidate is taking care of himself or herself emotionally.

Studies found that when people tell the truth, they provide longer, believable answers without much hesitation. Less smiling and body shifting are also seen as measures of believability. In one study, the single best predictor of truth was based on the plausibility of an answer. Meaning, if the content or meaning of a person's response "made sense," a truth judgement was found. Based on the aforementioned list, studies found that observers were less sensitive to idiosyncratic patterns and deviations from them than thought.

Verbal statements tend to be the most readily available source of information about a candidate and, at the same time, the least reliable in that verbal statements are easily controlled and able to be altered. It is difficult to constantly watch both verbal and nonverbal candidate cues. Many are missed over time.

Liars also control the obvious cues of speech and facial movements. These are fairly easy for the seasoned liar. Specific to speech, added pausing and a slightly higher pitch may be noticed; whereas, with the face, one might pick up on a different type of eye gazing and smiling as hints. Liars will adjust their behaviors and may try to avoid "dishonest" actions, making it more difficult to spot deception. Knowing that smiling and looking at someone are expected of an honest person, a liar may stare at you, smile, and lie right through their teeth. That's easy for a shrewd fabricator.

When the motivation for a politician to lie is high, nonverbal deceptive cues are greater than speech cues. And, as deceptive skills are developed and refined, the liar may tend to enjoy social interactions. He or she may see a get-together or party as an opportunity to test out his or her perfected deceptive behaviors and words without being caught. This banter actually excites the deceiver. High stakes lying involves the active appearance of looking credible and avoiding getting caught. A lot of thought and planning may go into this process. Strategies from a savvy liar even include countermeasures. Yet, a sophisticated liar will also know how to handle these strategies in order to remain undetected.

Discovering a lie is a process, especially in the early stage of a lie. This is like being suspicious of someone, but we are not quite sure why . . . just yet. And, based on Novotny and others' (2018) research on deception and nonverbal cues, we must remember that "no single cue has been linked firmly to deception." It's more like the "trusting your gut" feeling.

There is a difference between discovering a lie and suspecting a lie. This is a two-step process. Suspicion requires behavioral evidence, including verbal and nonverbal behaviors. On the other hand, discovery requires physical evidence, including third party information like confessions, physical evidence, or inconsistencies.

According to Novotny and others (2018), "The single most important factor when someone suspected a lie was based on behavioral evidence." We look for how they behave which is directly linked to the use of verbal and nonverbal cues. And we suspect a lie based on a trigger. Something triggered us to take notice. Our amygdala emotional trigger flipped on. We felt something and we seek to know more.

This is different than non-behavioral evidence which is defined as the use of third party information, confessions, physical evidence, and inconsistencies with prior knowledge. We use this type of evidence for the discovery phase of a suspected lie. The University of Michigan study (Mihalcea, 2015) on common lying behaviors found that:

- Thirty percent of liars scowled or grimaced their whole face
- Seventy percent looked directly at their questioner
- Forty percent gestured with both hands

An increase in *um* fillers was also found as well as the use of "he or she" versus "I or me" in order to distance the deceiver from the deceptive story being told.

When asked about suspicion in one study, volunteers were "more likely to report nonverbal/verbal behaviors over harder evidence" (Mihalcea, 2015). Yet, we must remember that we are not good at catching lies.

House Minority Leader Nancy Pelosi, conducts her weekly news conference.

When people see or feel a change in a person's behavior, this then triggers the need to push for more behavioral evidence. So, when we suspect a lie, we turn to discovery evidence or clues to either confirm or deny. In turn, this could lead to the discovery of a lie. When a candidate says a lie, he/she gives less plausible, shorter answers with longer latencies. Meaning, he or she speaks less with greater breaks in time before speaking again. We tend to believe physical evidence, third party information, direct confessions, and inconsistencies; or a combination of all of these factors in order to determine if someone is, in fact, lying.

There are two rules associated with when to lie: the "ulterior motive" rule and the "controllability" rule. The **ulterior motive rule** is when we see obvious self-serving behavior and we do not believe it. It's when someone has a hidden reason for doing something. It's negative and usually only benefits the person expressing it. Deception can easily be imbedded in this motive since it serves the liar.

The **controllability rule** is when we believe a person's performance based on the behaviors the candidate is least likely to deliberately and consciously control. If a person cannot control his or her behavior, then he/she cannot fake it. For this, we tend to look at difficult-to-control behaviors. Simply said, it's "the leaks" from the body and tone that automatically happen. Controllability and automaticity are variables specific to emotions and behavior. According to Ekman, "When emotion is aroused certain changes occur in the face, body, and voice which can be considered automatic."

Druckman and Bjork (1991) provide fascinating information about lying, leaking, and being revealed:

> Automatic links present a problem for deceivers who attempt to control their nonverbal behavior during deception: they must override these links in order to avoid leakage. Some nonverbal cues are more likely to be controlled than others. Words and facial expressions have been found to be easier to control than body and tone of voice cues. Thus, deceivers should be most successful when using words, next most successful when using facial expressions, and least successful when using body movements and tone of voice cues. Evidence on detection, both body cues and tone of voice cues are found to be more revealing than facial cues.

This is part of the concept of using a lie-detector machine. Assuming that a lie includes the fear of being caught or keeping secretive information, some degree of stress is evident. This emotional shift of these nonverbal physical changes in the body would then be captured by the lie detector.

Paul Ekman's work has shown that the average observer can pick up on actors who are "experiencing pleasant emotions or unpleasant ones when they viewed the actor's bodies, hands, and feet." However, this was not true when the observer only looked at the actor's face and head because the actor used a higher pitched voice and fewer hand movements when lying.

All persons, subconsciously, have an understanding of deceptive behaviors. And, when you know what to look for by distinguishing between important behavioral and non-behavioral clues, you might be able to catch a lie. I suggest you be vigilant in both watching and listening; record a debate and watch it a couple of times to see changes in baseline behaviors. Watch the candidates' emotional outbursts and how they behave/react with spilt screen camera shots. Refer to the context of the subject being debated and how candidates manage their facial expressions. Look for the motivation to lie. What's in it for that person?

Focus more on the intent to lie rather than active and impulsive lying. Vrij, Granhag, and Porter (2010) offer a good definition about targeting the liar's intent in that, "[a] successful attempt, without forewarning, is to create in another a belief which the communicator considers to be untrue."

Lie detectors can only catch so much; the fact is that good liars are proficient at lying. One research project clustered the assumptions that it is hard to detect a lie into three basic reasons:

1. Our lack of interest to probe into the questionable liar. Seriously, how much time do you want to invest in political issues?
2. Our limited understanding of basic lie detection standards and cues. You're not a detective studying human behavior.
3. We make common mistakes in trying to figure it out in our quest to get the truth. To muddy this, liars often embed truths in their lies, making it even more challenging for a truth-seeker.

One simple way to attempt to uncover deception deals with gathering information from the liar. An accusatory approach probably will not work. Look at politicians who have been caught lying. When hammered by the media, they will deny, deny, deny with a sense of urgency and defiance. However, when a news interviewer asks questions and gathers information from the suspected liar, this gives the liar a better chance at getting caught up in his or her own lies. Also, it is important to ask questions that the liar may not see coming.

One strategy employed by the liar is to imbed the lies in truths. By slipping a lie into a string of truths, it appears more believable. Telling is blatant lie is much harder than telling a truthful story and imbedding a lie or changing details here and there. One study suggested that lies imbedded in strong truthful statements may be laden with high-quality details in order to ensure believability from the receiver. Just as a truthful story has a lot of details, a good liar will do the same by strengthening the lie with lots of juicy details that we want to believe.

Remember President Bill Clinton. He clearly said that he did not have "sexual relations with that woman, Miss Lewinsky." Note that his rehearsed statement referenced Lewinsky first as "that woman." Anyone could be "that woman." He disassociated himself from her verbally and emotionally. Only then did he mention her by a formal title. During later questioning by the Independent Counsel's Office, Clinton stated, "I have never had sexual relations with Monica Lewinsky." Think about that. How do you define "sexual relations?" It almost sounds like a relationship and, clearly, Clinton was married and already in a relationship with his wife.

Later, when pressed, Clinton stated, "I thought the definition included any activity by [me], where [I] was the actor and came in contact with those parts of the bodies" which had been explicitly listed (and "with an intent to gratify or arouse the sexual desire of any person"). Note the subtle twisting of words. See how he manipulated the use of space, body terms, actions, and his place in all of that. He clearly attempted to position himself on the fray while distancing himself by using sly verbal tactics. The bottom line is that he defined "sexual relations" but spinning the contact with body parts and was even 'the actor.' Really? Yes, a good actor.

Watch tapes of him speaking about this subject with his wife Hillary Clinton often in the background or "by his side." You'll catch Bill shaking his finger at the camera to make his point while maintaining lots of eye contact for believability. He even holds tightly to the podium as if it protects him.

The photo below tells a lot about Hillary's feelings. While the couple is surrounded by fans and security, her covered eyes—while no one else is wearing sunglasses—lets us know she is hiding behind her Foster Grants. Bill's amused smile with lots of eye contact says one thing, but Hillary's pursed mouth while looking away tells a completely different story. I encourage you to look at old video footage and pictures to gain an understanding as to how leaders deceive and lure us in.

Look at the acting skills of a highly educated lawyer. Lawyers even have classes in law school about reading jurors' body language. They have clear insight as to how others think and feel in a variety of situations. Good actors are attuned with the emotional and psychological states of others. They believe it's their job to know how their lies will be received. They must know this.

There are no hard rules or cues specific to lying and body language. No single cue exists to consistently determine if someone is lying. Gestures and cues shift from person to person. We look for a person's words to align with prescribed emotions. For example, when talking about an attack on someone, we look for the victim to act and talk like a victim. Their emotions must match their words and the tone for us to believe. We must use caution as to not apply stereotypical nonverbals to people too quickly and judge them as deceptive. It's not that easy.

Specific to lying and nonverbals, several studies found that liars do not show nervousness or anxiety even with cognitive loads. Their nonverbals are subtle. However, you may embark on a quest to get down to truths and lies by focusing on elements of the demands of lying and brain impact. Vrij, Granhag, and Porter (2010) offer six strategies that will not call out a liar but may enhance the differences in cognitive loads between liars and truthful people. The lying brain uses more energy; specifically,

1. Liars have to remember their stories, the details, and be able to recall the deceptive points consistently as to not set off an alarm;
2. Liars know they are lying and need to self-check their behaviors to ensure that they are calm and transparent just like truth tellers;
3. Liars are constantly trying to read the person hearing the lie to make sure they are successful with all of their planned deception;
4. Liars know they are acting and, like most good actors, have to remind themselves to play the part;

5. Liars may know the truths of something and need to bury them to let the falsities surface. This is demanding on the thinking brain; and

6. Being intentional about lying requires mental effort. Liars have to think about it along with every other detail I mentioned earlier.

That makes for a heavy cognitive load. It takes a lot of sustained energy to lie.

Touching briefly on the scary realm of pathological liars and psychopaths in general, lying is part of their modus operandi; they have a history steeped in frequent and repeated lying without apparent motives or benefits. They just spontaneously and impulsively lie. Many just can't help themselves. Pathological liars and psychopaths have limited emotional capacities; thereby, making it even more difficult to figure out if they are lying. They fail to adhere to the same set of truth and lie standards. They even have the capacity to actually believe what they are saying. And of course, without guilt or fear. Over time, these lies even take on a "false belief" system. Meaning, their lies become truths in their minds.

In light of today's hot political election and current president, Donald Trump, the question of his truthfulness is under the microscope. Every president is under such scrutiny. For President Trump, the number of alleged lies or fake truths makes the daily news. A Google search on June 19, 2019 revealed claims that "President Trump has made 10,796 false or misleading claims in 869 days," as per the *Washington Post*. CNN Politics says that "Donald Trump has now said more than 10,000 untrue things as president." And that's not the big story.

Politifact even goes so far as to dissect President Trump's statements and then reveal the truth about each questionable statement—or lie (https://www.politifact.com/personalities/donald-trump/statements/byruling/false/). Check it out; honestly, check and recheck everything you hear and read in today's fake news environment. And notice how many politicians will reference lies as "not being truthful" or "inaccurate." When, in reality, it is lying—use the word. Plain and simple.

However, the old adage of "fool me once, shame on you; fool me twice, shame on me" may have some merit because receivers of lies often fail to learn from their mistakes. We want to believe someone, particularly someone we like and trust. Some surmise that it was a one-time thing, or that it would never happen again. Perhaps this is true; I suggest not.

Remember, as well, that each of us has our own baseline and views of deception and lying. Lying, a moral and ethical behavior, has numerous interpretations. White lies. Fibs. Name it what you like, but it definitely has a role in politics, viewpoints, and how we navigate society. Our emotional threshold and history with lying and liars skews how we interpret others who lie or exhibit falsities. Micro expressions and shifts in the tone of voice are not normal expressions and our ability to spot them is certainly not seen as vital for believable politicians.

Don't vote for a candidate because you like him or her "enough." Enough of that. I challenge you to not let the suspicion of deception pass by. While you shouldn't jump too quickly to a conclusion based on a single cue, you should watch nonverbals, like blink rates and micro expressions, to discover fact vs. fiction. Both visual and verbal information must match. Remember, a good liar is in control and knows you well. Your motive may be to vote for the best and most qualified candidate. A deceptive politician's motive is much different. Consider yourself warned.

"You can fool some of the people all of the time, and all of the people some of the time, but you cannot fool all of the people all of the time."
— Abraham Lincoln

CHAPTER 6

Reading Body Language: Being Intentional with Nonverbals while Being Under the Political Microscope

Both Ekman and Mehrabian confirm that, "most leaders focus on the verbal message and, according to the data, nonverbal message is equally, if not more, important." This is an understatement—it's much more important. We use body language to reinforce our message, affirm impressions of ourselves, model social behavioral expectations, and establish relationships. Nonverbal behaviors influence others. How we display our body language persuades others and gives the perception that we are in control of ourselves while conforming to societal expectations. It's a big deal.

Through a series of studies, well-known psychologist Albert Mehrabian's pioneering work found that approximately seven percent of how we communicate is verbal, thirty-eight percent is tone of voice, and approximately fifty-five percent is via our body language. Known as the "7-38-55 Rule," Mehrabian and others' research continuously reaffirms the strength of nonverbal communication in how we engage with other people. An overwhelming ninety percent+ of how we communicate with others comes from our body messages and through the tonal delivery of words.

Specific to the fifty-five percent+ of how we communicate with our nonverbals, body cues include:

- Body positions (sitting, standing, walking, gait, etc.)
- Gestures
- Touch
- Facial expressions

Specific to our thirty-eight percent +/- of our paralinguistic or tone of voice cues, we watch and listen for things like:

- Pitch, rate, tone of voice, silences, laughs, screams, sighs
- Pauses and gaps
- Increased or decreased rate of speech
- Monotone delivery

Other ancillary, but body language-related nonverbals include:

- Smells (study of haptics)
- Use of space (study of proxemics)
- Use of colors
- Use of objects, items, and emblems
- Artifacts (accessories like hats, watches, scarves, bags)

First impressions matter as well. Schiller et al. (2009) confirms that social information is encoded in our brains and forms impressions. It's fast, too. "When required to rapidly judge others, we appear to be efficient evaluators." Tied to our brain's emotional center, the amygdala, these impressions are tightly connected with our biases, as well. Meaning, we like what we like, and it's not necessarily based on truth or science. We can be a fickle bunch.

Yet, we should consider the power of first impressions based on what we see when first exposed to someone—in particular, political candidates or leaders who pique our initial interest. Whether positive or negative, lasting impressions will be made. We automatically watch for how they shake hands, get physically close to others, make eye contact, and exhibit different facial expressions. These nonverbal cues, along with several others, tell us about political candidates. Communication happens, even when words aren't part of the judgment.

Terms like submissive, trustworthy, powerful, and suspicious are connected to us emotionally, but how do they come across nonverbally? Our brains almost instantly determine "yes" or "no" for each condition presented to us. Trust may be the biggest deal. Trustworthiness actually takes just a couple of seconds. Meaning, the second you meet someone, you know whether or not to trust her or him.

It is difficult, if not impossible, to suppress all nonverbals, including unintentional behaviors ("the tell"). A politician must be more disciplined under the microscope to control behaviors and body movements. A nervous wiggle of the finger or chewing on the lip can quickly elicit a response from viewers. Similar to reputation, a political candidate's image is stamped on voters' brains, both emotionally and critically. Image and control are imperative for success.

Specific to making a first impression, nonverbal cues are multiple times more important than other cues. Goman (2018) suggests that they have four times the impact than other cues. Politicians should be highly aware of every signal. Everyone is watching.

Personal space (proxemics), physical gestures, posture, facial expressions, and eye contact are important variables associated with leadership. Studies on "looking Republican or Democrat," which were based on permanent features (bone structure and height) versus transitory features (head tilt, expressions, body positioning), showed that transitory features are less important than permanent ones.

Permanent facial features are a part of facial stereotyping, indicating what a "strong candidate" is supposed to look like. They include features like bone structure and components that cannot be modified. Whereas, transitory features can be altered. For example, head tilting and expressive eyebrows can be intentionally manipulated.

Leaders should always take heed as to their nonverbal communique, including how they sit, stand, walk, and gesture. There are distinct cues for eliciting confidence, competence, and status. This also holds true for stereotypical communal and agentic traits.

Research suggests that when the news media personalizes social issues using ordinary people "like you and me," citizens are ripe for engaging in the political arena. Consider how the media covers candidates during live interviews, as well as what clips they opt to air to draw viewing audiences in. Rich in content, these visual displays of candidates' verbal and nonverbal behaviors resonate with us, the viewers. Powerful nonverbals that we observe without really thinking about it include facial expressions, particularly the eyes and mouth, and the movements of the body. The subtle leaning in, eye contact, and controlled hand gestures of Representative Alexandria Ocasio-Cortez during a discussion in 2019 confirmed interest.

Positive cues, or engagement signals, include head nodding, leaning in, face-to-face alignment, and open body movements. The length of eye contact, or gazing, also increases. Visual cues and clues evoke both cognitive and emotional responses.

A sharp politician uses eye contact to their advantage by conveying credibility and control. Those who look at their opponents on the stage are perceived as more intelligent. Candidates who look head on when listening to a question appear more genuine. Control of the facial muscles around the eyes is an important means of captivating us, either in person or from the TV screen.

Alexandria Ocasio-Cortez attends the 2019 Athena Film Festival closing night film, *Knock Down the House.*

One French study finds that a strong visual strategy includes the use of large, close-up photos of politicians on their campaign materials. These close-up shots lend a more personal feel between candidate and viewer. During face-to-face interactions, we consider a politician's tone of voice, rhetoric, body position, use of gestures, and other nonverbals to persuade us. We are constantly watching to see what happens and how things look to us.

Looks matter. How we look plays a role in how we are treated and perceived. Face, hair, makeup, glasses, and gestures of the head are important. Numerous studies confirm that the more physically attractive someone is, the better he/she is evaluated by others. And, this applies to politicians, as well. One cannot separate politicians and how they look. Perceptions are powerful and politicians' visual personas leave lasting impressions.

Focusing on the technical elements of an image, visuals also include how people are portrayed through lenses. Meaning, what do we see within the frame of the TV or photograph that captures us and leaves an impression? Candidates and their strategists must purposely decide what an image, photograph, or television set should look like from the audience's point of view. From the angle of the camera to the type of lighting, these technical elements leave an imprint on us as to what we feel and think. A particular relationship occurs simply by watching the candidate or studying the photograph.

When looking at photos or television images, we absently notice what else is in the image. For example, flags indicate patriotism. In America, the symbolism of flags is important. Think about a time when you watched a president signing something behind his desk in the Oval Office. What did you see? Who did you see? From the drapes to the mahogany desk and type of pen used, these visual markers enhance the image and are seared in your brain.

Other examples include the use of images like podiums and props. We notice when the political figure is hiding behind the wooden podium versus being seen through a plexiglass stand. As we watch candidates consume their space, we take in how they stand, walk, move around the room, and interact with the audience or even the camera. It is imperative for American political figures to make eye contact. We demand it to determine trust, interest, and authenticity. One study suggested that people look at gestures and facial expressions the most to determine the tone or feeling of what they saw.

THE BODY LANGUAGE OF POLITICS ★ 137

US Senator Kamala Harris greets attendees during the SF Pride Parade on June 30, 2019.

Let's look at Democratic candidate Senator Kamala Harris and her nonverbals during a campaign event in San Francisco in June 2019. Study this photo. What do you see? How does the image resonate with you? Allow me to point out some obvious body language:

- Choice of clothing: In this case, a Pride rainbow jacket.
- Hair: Pulled up and casual to look like others in the audience. "I'm just like you."
- Eye contact: Lots of it.
- Hands: Ready to physically connect with people.

- Her body position: She turns to interact with the supporters.
- Others in the image: Acceptance of diversity.

Spouses and families in photos or news clips also tell viewers that family is important. From childhood photos to sports or college memories, images reinforce what a candidate wants you to know about her or him.

When focusing on candidates and image management, we see a lot. We also notice if the spouse or family are included and how they are positioned. What is everyone wearing? Do their smiles look authentic or forced? Does the camera display close up shots of them? Researchers point out that above-eye level shots are 'less favorable' than below angles. Meaning, the degree of the camera angle has an impact on how we judge someone. Magazines have made millions with this knowledge.

We notice a myriad of things—all at the same time—in order to judge what we think we see. Important aspects to consider when looking at political photos or video clips include:

1. **Objectives/Manipulations:** What objects do we see in the frame? For example, former President Obama replaced the Winston Churchill statue in the Oval Office with one of Martin Luther King. A bowl of fruit can soften the look of a room while encouraging people to gather around.
2. **The physical environment:** How big is the crowd? What's the shape of the room? We quickly identify the Oval Office. How does our leader interact with his or her surroundings?
3. **Status:** Where does the leader sit in relationship to others in the room? Does she stand or sit? Does he command the chair? Is that chair made of leather? Is our leader hiding behind the podium?

4. **Sense of time:** Does our leader wear a watch? Are they known for being on time? We associate feelings of consideration with how people treat time.
5. **Colors:** We have specific colors for events and status. For example, academics wear blue robes. Brides wear white. Yellow makes us feel warm and cozy. Red emanates power. Blue transmits trust and faith.

Nonverbal cues help define our views of a candidate and research confirms that these traits are "reliable predictors of candidate viability and success" (Gong & Bucy, 2016). When candidates go against nonverbal behavior expectations, we punish them for misbehaving and breaking from social norms and unspoken behavioral expectations. We see it and we hear it. When verbal rhetoric competes with inappropriate nonverbal leader displays, we have a hard time cognitively processing the verbiage. Visual nonverbals consume us more.

Bucy's (2016) study of bad body language, also known as nonverbal expectancy violations, confirms that we judge actions as positive, negative, or neutral. Positive nonverbals include a welcoming tone of voice, attentive eye movements, appropriate touch, and open body language. Negative violations, on the other hand, may include an unwelcome aggressive tone, over-touching, unexpected defensive body movements, and belligerent facial expressions. Neutral body language show arms at one's side and relaxing hands with displayed palms. The candidate's facial expressions are relaxed; no prominent veins are seen, and the skin color isn't blanched or splotchy.

Three primary facial displays studied by Bucy and others found that successful politicians must master and control happiness and reassurance; anger and anxiety; and fear and evasion. All of these attributes hold hidden meanings. Happiness and reassurance lessen aggression and diminish hostility. Anger and anxiety signal action and defense. Fear and evasion spark retreat. Regardless of your political favorites, look at the following politicians' facial displays. What do you see that a photographer captured and wanted us to see? Even the selection of these particular photos is guided by what I want you to see.

Donald Trump speaks during the Presidential Debate at Hofstra University on September 26, 2016.

Senator Amy Klobuchar listens to testimony during a Senate Commerce Subcommittee on Aviation and Space hearing about the current state of airline safety.

Kamala Harris delivers a keynote address during a Safer Internet Day event at Facebook headquarters on February 10, 2015.

When candidates display happiness and reassuring facial (and gesture) movements, viewers are apt to support them, and their popularity subsequently increases. Supporters like to see positive displays, while critics jump on the negative displays. One exception, though, is that both supporters and critics do not respond well to fear and evasion displays. These expressions and behaviors weaken a candidate and bring up questions about his or her leadership.

Tics are repetitive actions performed by a candidate under stress or heightened anxiety; these might include lip licking, lip compression, tongue movements around the mouth, squinting, jaw clenching, sniffling, throat clearing, coughing, shrugging, and neck bending or titling. These are usually involuntary actions and serve to self soothe the candidate.

Mitch McConnell speaks to the media after attending the Republican weekly policy luncheon on June 4, 2019.

Based on the aforementioned photos, we also can accurately guess tone of voice, solely based on their body language. A leader who wants to display an image of power uses tonal and style elements like pauses and pitch when speaking or using verbal messaging. For example, when a seven-second pause was used during a suspicious questioning activity, the pause increased suspicion. When pausing was used after a self-serving statement by a candidate, it was seen as a lie. It is as though the pause was needed for the listener to absorb the truth of what was just said. Both positive and negative nonverbals have been studied to determine the mental condition of someone. The table below summarizes a slew of actions:

Action/Behavior	Positive	Negative
Tone of voice	Upbeat, hopeful	Threatening, menacing
Gestures	Affinity (bonding)	Defiant (aggressive)
Blink rate	At/Near baseline rate	Increased or glaring (slower)
Tics	Nodding, quick smiles	Jaw clenching, lip licking
Body status	Open arms/legs, torso relaxed	Arms/Legs crossed, torso stiff
Skin	Colored, smooth, natural	Blanched, sweaty, blotchy

In contrast, when a seven-second pause was used during a truthful statement, the pause only increased the believability of the statement. This aligns with the adage that "silence is powerful" and should perhaps be mastered. When listening to the nonverbal latency, or pausing, think about how this impacts you. For example, during President Trump's thirteen-second pause at a July 2019 rally, the "send her back" chant quickly went viral and created controversy.

Additionally, we know there is a relationship between a candidate's pitch, as part of voice tone, and election outcomes. Findings suggest that both men and women prefer their candidate to have a lower-pitched voice; this was even more important for female candidates. During studied debates and speeches, candidates with lower-pitched voices beat out their male opponents. Interestingly, when two females debated, the one with the higher-pitched voice triumphed.

Rhythm, pitch, monotonousness, softness, harshness, silence, and speed are also indicators of how someone is feeling or how that particular tone of voice is making someone else feel. In a political situation, the favorability of the speaker may "possibly increase with a strong voice tone and suitable stresses" (Demir, 2011). Voters prefer lower-pitched voices, and these candidates are picked more by both males and females.

Men with lower-pitched voices are also considered to be more attractive, physically stronger, and dominant. In interviewing candidates, "an air" of leadership is noted when the question is followed by a pause before answering.

Visual cues play a dominant role in affecting our responses during an audio/visual presentation. This pertains to both ordinary citizens and political candidates. This holds true regardless of socio-economic status for how people influence each other. Leaders tend to walk in the middle of a group or a couple of steps ahead. At tables, leaders take center and subordinates flank out in terms of status, as well.

We are able to glean correct information in a fraction of a second using nonverbal cues. When people do not know a lot about a candidate or leader, they gather information from that person's body language.

Photographs have the ability to convey competence, integrity, and fitness for office. Now, imagine the ability to photoshop an image. When this is done, even on photos of human faces, it significantly alters our assessment of a candidate. By making wrinkles, scars, and extra skin magically disappear, a politician looks more youthful and healthier.

When a candidate has a powerful message, this is associated with being "strong and valid." Imagine the charisma of a powerful presenter. You may or may not remember what that person said, but you can clearly recall how that person acted. We remember their brand. Perhaps you were even mesmerized by the way that they commanded the room and drew others in. Control of the presidential hopeful's image is important due to the impression he or she leaves on potential voters. Candidates always seek to be strong, likable, competent, and, of course, trustworthy.

The confident delivery of a speech with a strong message correlates with one's qualifications index, thereby increasing the chances of being elected. One's nonverbals have a stronger connection to being elected over one's qualifications. While qualifications may deem someone fit for office, the power between nonverbals and getting elected is important because visual cues affect perceived credibility, truthfulness, and how well-suited a politician is for office. Eye contact, particularly in the American culture, evokes feelings of openness, interest, and being genuine.

Lobinger and Brantner (2015) found that politicians use an "interplay between impression management strategies" and specific tricks and techniques that are performed by the media in order to control visual representation. These visual cues include: nonverbals specific to the body; technical elements like camera angles and closeups; and details of an image, like flags in the background. And, who doesn't have a flag in the background!

Image techniques include strategies for self-promotion, ingratiation, intimidation, and exemplification. While a candidate may be able to control the majority of his or her nonverbal behaviors, control from the media and, specifically, camera and media tactics, are most likely not in their control.

Visual imagery specific to nonverbal behavior may include how the candidate dresses, uses facial expressions, gestures, and interacts with others. Friendly body movements include touching a person, firm handshakes, leaning in, a nonsexual touch or hug, and nodding the head. Specific nonverbal cues help people with understanding someone's social status and they include voice pitch, facial appearance, nonverbal gestures, attractiveness, and physical size. In addition to attractiveness, body shape matters, as previously discussed. I bring it up again because we, the masses, hold the contradictory views that "bigger is better" and that "fat is bad." People are naturally drawn to men of larger stature; though not so much for women. Research even confirms that taller professionals are recruited faster and paid more in the workplace. Since 1900, the taller candidate has won nineteen of twenty-eight presidential elections.

The muscularity of a person also has implications of how people perceive leaders. The physical appearance of a body with muscle tone boils down to a mixture of nutrition, hormones, and physical exercise for most bodies. Those with impressive physiques work hard to achieve that physical condition. This, too, can serve as a signal of status following along the line of bigger is better.

Taller people are viewed as higher in status and more leaderlike solely based on their height. Some researchers have questioned if the West's choices of men in leadership roles is due to the fact that they are taller than women. Overall, people expect taller people to be more successful in our society.

Independent mayoral candidate Bo Dietl, Mayor Bill de Blasio and Republican mayoral candidate Nicole Malliotakis on Wednesday, November 1, 2017.

We actually give male leaders perceived "extra height." They might even be larger than life. Whereas, opponents, regardless of actual height, are assigned shorter status because of how we feel toward them. A look at the final 2017 mayoral debate between candidate Bo Dietl, Bill de Blasio, and Nicole Malliotakis shows extreme height differences between the three candidates. In the end, de Blasio won. Could height have played a role in voters' perceptions?

McCann (2001) stated that "even the US presidential election outcome is partially predicted by height of the winning candidate." Research confirms that taller individuals are viewed as higher in status and more dominant. They are also more apt to be assigned the leader role. We assign taller people traits like competence, charisma, and intelligence (Blaker and van Vugt, 2014). Do you remember five-foot-five Ross Perot? Could this have influenced the outcome?

Additionally, taller women are perceived as assertive, affluent, and ambitious, but not as attractive when compared to taller men. Silventoinen (2003) found that eighty percent of height is based on genetic factors and twenty percent comes from environmental factors. With access to nutritious food and limited health issues or sickness, individuals can develop better. People who grow up in wealthy, privileged conditions usually reach their full height potential because of access to food, exercise, and emotional connections. Therefore, height may be an "honest signal" of status. People notice taller people. Studies confirm that taller people get noticed and promoted more quickly at work as well.

Numerous studies have also found that height is associated with intelligence and brain activity, particularly in Western cultures. Blaker and Vugt (2014) conducted an online study and concluded that "taller men and women were judged to be more intelligent than their shorter counterparts, as well as more dominant, healthy, and leaderlike." Another study found that taller women were viewed as more intelligent, as well.

Studies show that in a society in which food is readily available, it is culturally frowned upon for one to be obese. In our society, we often link it to lower socioeconomic status because fresh, healthy, and organic food is expensive. People who struggle for food security can primarily only afford high fat, highly processed inexpensive food, which leads to weight gain. Those with economic resources—the wealthy—have a healthy diet. This is not the case for other countries but holds true in the Western culture.

Obesity is an open target for discrimination and judgment. One's stature and how they carry themselves is powerful, along with broad shoulders and wide body displays. Those with leaner, more muscular bodies devoid of large deposits of fat are also perceived as bigger in a positive way specific to leadership. Check out the photo of world Heads of State from the G7 meeting in Quebec, Canada on June 8, 2018. Status, fitness, and space consumption are obvious.

(left to right) European Union Council President Donald Tusk, British Prime Minister Theresa May, German Chancellor Angela Merkel, US President Donald Trump, Canadian Prime Minister Justin Trudeau, French President Emmanuel Macron, Japan Prime Minister Shinzo Abe, Italian Prime Minister Giuseppe Conte, and European Union Commission President Jean-Claude Juncker.

Different body shapes elicit different feelings from us. Muscular bodies are perceived as adventurous and healthy. Thin, lean bodies are perceived as quieter or tenser. And, fuller, rounder bodies are assigned as lazy or socially unacceptable. Body size is one prejudice that is still openly fair game in today's world of political correctness. Even during the slightest conflict, most defensive and aggressive fighters will attempt to weaken their foes by attacking physical appearances. Either perceived or real, these behaviors are perpetuated as we look for clues to fit our constructs.

We will actually study a face for cues when we do not have a sufficient amount of knowledge about the candidate. Meaning, looks matter. We must read a face for information, regardless of the words coming from that face/politician. Micro expressions—the quick little facial movements we all make—produce valuable insights as to what others are thinking and feeling. A candidate's perceived personality can come through facial expressions. Conservative voters tend to pick up on the "look" of their preferred candidate. Research says we like:

- Wide cheekbones
- High eyebrows
- Wide pupils
- Noses that are not too long or too narrow
- Full heads of hair
- Certain hair color for women (Do blondes really have more fun? Umm, no.)
- Little or no facial hair for men
- Big symmetrical smiles

Our faces produce thousands of different movements: precise meaning is provided for the receiver from each different movement. Look at the variations for each facial part and you can confirm that reading body language is a taxing job!

When examining nonverbals and confidence, nonverbal dimensions triumph over a politician's message. Nonverbal markers are used to pick up confidence clues such as elements of the voice, tone, and positioning of the body. Facial features immediately evoke a response from a viewer as he or she seeks to understand what the displayed nonverbals mean. One study found that children as young as three could recognize cues of confidence when watching adults give instructions.

In addition to eyes enhancing communication, they also secretly tell us the health of candidates. No one likes to see bloodshot eyes staring back at them. We know a healthy person has bright, clear scleras, or the whites of the eyes. When we see red or bloodshot eyes, we internally ask ourselves, *Did they stay up too late? Are they hungover? Do they allergies? Do they do drugs?* The eyes speak loudly without saying a word.

Smiling is one of the only facial expressions that is universal. Almost everyone knows what a smile means and can judge whether or not it is sincere or fake. Smiles are a quick, welcoming gesture.

Smiling candidates, compared to those who do not smile in public or on campaign materials, receive more votes. Smiling conveys immediate nonverbal meaning. Research finds that food servers who smile receiver bigger tips, smilers are trusted more quickly, and smiling exudes confidence. On the flip side, mouth displays that evoke negative feelings from us include smirking, excessive smiling, and mouths in which one side is lifted from the other—like a feeling of disgust—or smirk.

Donald Trump makes a face during a cabinet meeting on July 16, 2019.

Facial morphology influences outcomes and we make quick judgments based on appearance.

Sarcasm looks like a slight downcast smile in which the mouth is no longer symmetrical, and we are sensitive to this. A contraction of the eye or eyes makes us take notice. If someone even scratches the nose or brow, we question what's going on with that candidate. Whatever the nonverbal, we catch through visual sources. We notice.

Research examining the use of facial poses found that the left cheek is displayed more often than the right cheek. This left-forward choice solicited a more emotional appeal to viewers in numerous studies. Further, emotions tend to be more expressive when shown with the left side of the face. Remember school photos and how we were positioned for the camera. Political photos are no different. They are staged and the angle of the face is intentional to elicit a response from viewers. One case examined the use of head poses in four countries, including the US. In all four results, the left face display won compared to right or center display. In the US, forty-eight percent posed left, twenty-eight percent right, and twenty-four percent center (Thomas, et al., 2012).

Experts found that conservative politicians displayed the left cheek in order to appear more emotionally expressive and connect with viewers. Since research confirms that females tend to be drawn to this without even thinking, this is quite a clever way to draw an audience. Data on facial side use found that sixty-four percent of conservatives used leftward poses compared to fifty-four percent of liberal politicians. Interestingly, more females (thirty-six percent) displayed a front forward face display compared to male (twenty percent) photos. Specific to party affiliation, liberal candidates were more likely to face forward than conservative candidates in photographs.

Perhaps women intentionally face the camera to reduce the use of emotions and present the perception that they are "facing" any situation head on. Given the communal traits expected of women, including being emotional, not tilting the head would give the perception of reducing emotions.

We know that tilting the head ever so slightly is a female non-verbal gesture. A highly-polished candidate will try to ensure that her face and pose strike the right feelings of connectedness with viewers. Regardless, dominant nonverbal male features, like a strong jaw or pronounced brow, are preferred by most voters. Men and women want dominant-looking faces from their candidates. Yet, women with dominant features are not found attractive and could be penalized for being "manly." Former Attorney General Janet Reno was scrutinized often. I urge you to withhold judgment in the voting booth.

It takes a lot of time to master all of the nonverbals used to convey a message even when some of these nonverbals are quick and easy to decipher. Studies found that a more effective leader creates an emotional connection with followers by including hand gestures. This was considered critical to success.

Goman's (2018) work stated that it takes an "average of three hours of continuous interaction to develop the same level or rapport that you get with a single handshake." Read that again. It's a big deal. Hand gestures affect followers. The more people use non-verbal immediacy, the more others see them in a positive manner and want to be around them. Shaking hands is one of the first times that strangers voluntarily touch each other. This nonverbal activity is critical for the first few seconds as recipients judge the size of the hand, position of the palms, pressure of the grip, length of the hold, location of the other hand, and overall role of the body.

Positive hand gestures include a show of the hands with palms exposed, hands clasped in front around the waist level, and hands steeped together with fingertips touching. In a public setting, negative hand gestures include hands in the pockets, armed crossed over the chest, and hands behind the back. A neutral position of the hands might be considered keeping the hands at one's side.

We actually rate people who use a greater variety of hand gestures move favorably in terms of warmth, agreeableness, and energy. To be more effective, a leader should understand the nuances of nonverbal behaviors and create immediacy with followers.

The use of the hands also extends the verbal message and can either support the body's other nonverbals or contest them. When candidates become excited or passionate about a topic, they tend to use large and consuming hand and arm movements. If hand gestures fail to support the spoken words, the overall picture is mismatched, and words are questioned. For example, a speaker talking about a successful project while wringing his hands sends a mixed message.

Common hand gestures we see displayed include location of the hands on or around the body, finger pointing, fist making, waving, and hand shaking. Each of these has both positive/affirming and negative/questioning meanings. For example, too much waving of the hands or shaking of the fingers elicits erratic or overenthusiastic thoughts. Finger pointing may feel like a spear going through its recipient. And, of course, hands with the palms pressing down, like quieting a room, quickly evoke images of Hitler's militaristic famous "Heil Hitler" pose. In the case of German Chancellor Angela Merkel waving to delegates in 2018, many may be sensitive and biased to the certain hand gestures and the feelings they evoke. Just a single shot can make us react.

German Chancellor and leader of the German Christian Democrats Angela Merkel waves to the delegates.

Agentic behaviors look aggressive, competitive, and even threatening. A few of these gestures include forceful arm movements, finger-pointing, fist shaking, assertively leaning forward, and thrusting one's body into the space of another. Power is definitely the image here. Hedonic behaviors strengthen social status and bond individuals. Gestures include waving hands, giving the thumbs up, nodding the head, and touching another person. This approach capitalizes on pleasing another and triggers emotions like love, joy, and satisfaction.

The use of intentional gestures is well documented and a source of communicating for reinforcing one's words. During the 2016 election, both Donald Trump and Bernie Sanders displayed aggressive use of their hands, arms, and fingers.

Different hand and arm positions produce different reactions from viewers. The horizonal use of arms are perceived as "emotionally stable" compared to vertical movements, which are found to be "less agreeable" and "dominant." A wide display of hands and arms elicits feelings of openness, both literally and figuratively; whereas, quick and repetitive hand and arm movements evoke feelings of instability or emotional upset.

Neuroscientists have examined the relationship between the spoken word and displayed gestures. They found that the message was lost when the gestures did not match what the leaders said. Gender and gestures reviews found that women were seen as having less leadership qualities if they used gestures considered dominant or aggressive. They did better if their nonverbals were more restrained.

The following is a list of hand/arm gestures and their meanings which are frequently displayed by politicians (Lefebre, 2011):

Gesture	Meaning
"V" made with two fingers with palm and fingers outward	Victory, success

Raise the hand with the index finger pointed up or a little higher	Beckoning, trying to get someone's attention
Thumbs up (closed hand thrust forward with thumb raised)	Everything is okay or fine
Nodding head up and down or back and forth	Signals yes/agreement or no/disagreement
Rolling the eyes	Amazement, disbelief, incredulity
Closed eyes	I don't want to see this
Cupping a hand around the ear	Unable to hear someone
Wrinkling or scrunching the nose	Dislike, disgust, disagreeable
Hand holding or stroking the chin	Contemplation, evaluation, in thought
Firm handshake with eye contact	Standard greeting to solicit trust

Much attention is given to how we display our arms. Axtell (1998) identified ways in which we communicate with our arms. Specific to candidates, the following are commonly displayed and what they might infer:

Arm Movement	Meanings
Arms folded/crossed in front of the body at chest	Defensive, cold, protected, baseline relaxed, reserved, nervous
Akimbo, hands on the hips with arms bent outward	Impatience, frustration, anger, curiosity, physically growing the body

Arms behind the back, hands clasped	Ease and control, exposing the torso demonstrating nothing to fear, military inference
Arms by side with hands in pockets	Hidden hands denote insecurity, trying to appear smaller
Arms at sides with hands loosely clasped or open at sides	Relaxed, neutral, emotionally in control
Hands clapping with raised arms	Praise and appreciation, faster includes greater enthusiasm or agreement
Arms raised with shaking the fist	Anger, opposition, aggressive
Pointed finger with outstretched arm	Rude, aggressive
Arms raised with hand outstretched; palm facing someone else	Impolite, "stop" action, a barrier between the other person and you, attempt to shutdown someone else, no

Demir's (2011) extensive work on nonverbal communication in politics yielded interesting body movements that can be associated with leaders. Specifically, our bodies move in three basic ways: open, closed, and at rest. Posturing of the body could be erect or slumped. Confident people move their bodies as part of communicating. For example, a display of arm movements with outstretched hands is common for a confident speaker. Closed behaviors include crossing of the body with crossed legs or arms. Even putting something in your mouth or chewing on a pencil or fingernail could unveil inner feelings.

Another study, called the Dr. Fox Lecture (1973), had an actor give an incoherent speech to several groups of educators and professionals. While the speech was riddled with contradictory information, the actor received favorable responses due to participants' perceptions of his relaxed manner, including his positive hand gestures. This has powerful implications. Bodies "talk." Posture, hands, and feet do not go unnoticed.

Specific to posture, how someone manipulates his or her space is important. The torso can be expanded, the hips may jut out, and the shoulders considered broad. Research from the Kellogg School of Management noted that "posture expansiveness" activated a "sense of power" from the subject and that subject actually behaved differently.

Nonverbal dominant displays, like taking up physical space or being loud, usually reward male candidates, but female candidates are punished for displaying these agentic actions. Leaning on a desk with hands griping or splayed across the desk are considered masculine displays. Check out the body language between these politicians (L to R): Pelosi, Pence, Trump, and Schumer during an Oval Office meeting. What do you read here? I see Trump sitting forward and talking with his hands to make his point. Pence is sitting back and completely disengaged. Schumer won't even look at Trump. Pelosi is talking to somebody off screen, perhaps a journalist while pointing her finger. There's a lot of unhappy discussions happening in this room.

Political status is considered big. To make one's status larger, consuming space is an obvious tactic. Making large hand gestures, moving the arms in air space, and displaying a wider stance are examples of growing one's body in a particular environment for a particular purpose.

Accessories also connect people with their leaders. We associate these body decorations as an extension of the person. For example, it's hard to forget President Teddy Roosevelt's round glasses. This iconic style of glasses resonates with people. Hillary Clinton's choice of clothing, grooming, and color choices are also memorable. The media's countless hours devoted to her pantsuits or latest hairstyle were splashed across headlines for months. Emotional reactions to music and voice type also play a role in how we feel towards a particular candidate.

Body language activates emotion. When voters are anxious, we will remember candidates' trait characteristics and nonverbal behaviors more than their respective political parties. We feel strongly about people who make us feel nervous or anxious. A candidate may look angry or flustered when finger pointing, fist making, head shaking, or rocking back and forth. In turn, we respond.

Researchers are able to code specific nonverbals and associate them with emotional responses. When Bucy (2015) investigated nonverbal behaviors exhibited during a candidate "losing" a debate, he documented several nonverbal actions associated with this: physical weakness, pronounced stress, fearful or evasive behaviors, and other external signs of subordinate behavior. Bucy noted verbal indicators as signs of losing, as well. The struggling candidate may show discomfort with camera angles or the besieging of questions by news anchors.

Group-based emotions are strong predictors as part of collective action with anger being the lead emotion for binding a group. Anxiety-laden voters use candidates' characteristics and nonverbal behaviors more than party affiliation and ideology when voting.

Emotionally charged news stories hook voters and evoke higher levels of participation. For example, when 2008 presidential hopeful McCain spoke about crime and included attack ads against then-candidate Barack Obama, the images had darkened backgrounds and skin tone editing—thereby, suggesting crime with "dark," either by overtones of skin or setting.

Both black and white candidates use racial messaging. However, the construction of these messages vary by the author or the message. When a black candidate's skin tone was intentionally made darker with advertising gimmicks, he or she received more negative evaluations.

In mixed color candidate races, studies found that white candidate ads included explicit appeals sixty-seven percent of the time compared to implicit appeals. More often, white ads also included less dynamic photographs of their black opponent—thereby, immediately drawing the viewer's attention to the opponent's race. Alongside a black image, white ads tended to include character attack messaging using stereotypes. For example, welfare and violent crime statistics were included on the ad as part of the white candidate's "promise" to tackle. Found in the research, "the relative absence of substantive issues in such ads heightens the degree of connection of race with the racial stereotype" (McIlwain and Caliendo, 2009).

Based on the research, black candidates tended to use racial appeal, but with a different logic. Black ads included more substantive issue content while also responding to or defending themselves against white attack ads. Black candidates used explicit appeals more than white candidates. Candidates from the North used explicit appeals more than Southern candidates. Black candidates also used racial appeals when running against black opponents. White candidates used "racial appeals to gain a competitive advantage over black candidates."

For example, let's look at the battle in 2000 for Alabama's seventh congressional district seat between incumbent Earl Hilliard (black) and candidates Artur Davis (black) and Sam Wiggins (white). Hilliard and Dave made claims of "racial authenticity" to appeal to the black majority of voters within their district. By bringing race into the formula for voters, it became part of the rationale for voting a particular way and, in no means, had anything to do with other qualifying factors.

We know facial images make for quick voter selections. Experts confirm that candidates' facial expressions and behavioral traits impact electoral success. Not surprisingly, candidate attractiveness remains a top contender. Fortunately, Stockemer and Praino (2015) suggest that educated voters will not use attractiveness cues when voting. Voters without political savvy, though, will reward a candidate's appearance.

Regardless, I encourage you to open your eyes and look at all of the factors, including your own biases, prejudices, and perceptions. Evidence suggests that when you have limited or no information about a candidate's views, you will default to nonverbal cues in your decision making. Fight this urge.

"Just because a feeling is natural does not mean it should be indulged."
—Roseanna White

CHAPTER 7

How to Make Informed Decisions with Your Vote: Justifying Your Choices

An image is body language and nonverbal amalgamated. Every detail counts when we look and listen to candidates. I urge you to understand and justify why you pick a certain candidate. There are clear-cut reasons.

As we try to make sense of our choices and our vote, we like to be in control. By being in charge, we are better able to handle our emotions, including fear, stress, and anxiety. The thought of the unknown keeps millions up at night. The fear of what could go wrong or what might happen often has dire consequences for our minds and bodies. So, being in control brings us a feeling of being at ease. Voting helps us believe we are in control.

The very nature of the voting process gives us options, even though we are constantly besieged with visuals designed to influence us. Just as we like to think we are in control of who wins the election, the media and clever strategists work tirelessly to persuade viewers to vote a certain way using a mix of perceptions and facts that saturate our brains and pick at our emotions.

Media outlets are prone to emphasizing candidates through nonverbal analyses and have no problem overemphasizing non-communal or aggressive behaviors. Campaign news strategies are keenly aware of the power of telling their viewers what to see and what should be interpreted from this. Some might even call this being spoon-fed by the media.

One study found that female candidates received more votes when they were calm, refined, and reserved. This was evident with male voters, in particular. Sadly, if a woman exhibits more forceful gestures, she might be viewed as "erratic and less competent" (Everitt, et al., 2016).

The ability to influence someone is powerful. Most people are smart. However, savvy people can also be manipulated. Barker (2019) offers ways in which we are persuaded, and this research shows the link between neuroscience and our brains. Interwoven with *The Influential Mind* (Sharot, 2017), research on how our brains process information, we operate from a belief system deeply imbedded in us. As we take in someone's body language, we judge it against our current belief systems, values, and preconceived notions to assess its relevance and importance. The "boomerang effect" happens when new information challenges our current constructs, thereby, thrusting us back to an original source of information as a challenge or disbelief. It's like a fight in our heads between this candidate or that candidate.

Emotions are powerful and deeply ingrained in our brains. This powerful, primitive system drives our feelings and, often, many of our decisions. Our brains like to be "in sync" emotionally as we build a rapport with another person. We yearn to connect with our political party and our favorite candidate. During turbulent polit-ical times, our emotions run high and we are either in sync or out of sync with other people over this subject. There is a common sense reason that we don't talk about "religion or politics."

When we are emotionally aligned with someone, we mirror body movements. When we share feelings, we bond. Our in-group is working for us—just like a political rally. We impact how others feel about us and how we feel about them. Emotions are at the surface . . . forging actions and words.

Influence and our natural curiosity are also at play, Meaning, when we don't know something, we might ask questions, study the subject, or investigate until we are "in the know." With new information constantly being thrown at us, we are forced to reorder storylines, create new pathways, and get answers for information that does not flow with our timelines. For example, when the news tells us a candidate served in the Peace Corps, we want to know when, why, and if that candidate kept the peace. Or, did this person enlist in lieu of serving one's country or after returning from overseas? One simple fact can lead our minds and curiosities through a maze until we reach a satisfactory answer.

Our state of mind also influences our emotions. Under threat or even the fear of threat, humans stay low and seek shelter. We seek to preserve ourselves so when exposed to negative information, our brains often go into hyperdrive in order to make sense out of something sensitive. Think of a national tragedy or a massive incident. We immediately think of safety and are concerned for the wellbeing of others and ourselves.

In terms of influencing voting choices, if there is a negative wrapped around change or even the perception of change, people tend to back away. We seek familiarity, even with our voting choices. You've heard it before: "Better to stay with the devil you know then the devil you don't." Sharot suggests that the hint of a bad consequence may be "more effective than promising rewards."

Different strategies are used to sway us, including the psychology of status. It is important for a candidate to control his or her status to appeal to a broad audience by intentionally controlling body language. We don't like a person who didn't earn his stripes or pay her dues. Additionally, few will follow someone with whom they share little and to whom they cannot relate. We know statuses are based on dominance hierarchies; they operate on fear, threat, control, and intimidation. We often see these unfavorable behaviors in politicians.

Some hierarchies are established by status, others by prestige. As Blaker and van Vugt (2014) point out, status is usually achieved by competition, winning, or losing; whereas, prestige is bestowed upon someone who can bring something to the group—perhaps a skill or strength that the group needs.

High-status individuals usually receive more submissive displays from "lower-ranking members," according to the research. Think about hierarchical entities: the military, government, corporations, and schools. All are rooted in this tiered structure in which status, rank, and treatment are based on position. Too often these systems use force, intimidation, and fear as basic operating principles. Remember the principal's office? Or, threat of government shutdown?

On the other hand, prestige is achieved by lower-ranking individuals who freely and willingly accept their place within the hierarchy. These individuals voluntarily align with the prestigious person because of what that person can bring to the group or them individually. Therefore, a democratic voting system appeals to us and our needs. We, the lower ranking individuals of America, willingly agree to follow a chosen politician because this person's nonverbal and verbal communication meets a need for us. President Trump's unwavering and loyal following meets the needs of millions as evidenced by their willingness to "drain the swamp," regardless of who's in the swamp.

Politicians spend hours talking about what they have and what our country needs. People's abilities to influence are powerful when they want them to be. As I mentioned earlier, people are drawn to power. It feels good to be in control and be a part of the winning team. If we align ourselves with a strong, confident person, we, too, are then confident by proxy. So, when candidates talk politics or act informed about critical issues, we jump on board and are influenced to take part. The rally or party convention concepts are perfect examples with dressing the part, chanting the songs, waving the flags, and clapping with the masses as if to say, "Look at me, I'm a part of this and it's a big deal."

How politicians are treated by the media impacts our perceptions of them, and when journalists ask tough questions, the stakes are raised for how candidates will respond. Of course, there are expectations that we have for candidates.

Let's examine the "ideal candidate" and the "populist candidate" to see if we are persuaded to blindly follow a particular type based upon their nonverbals.

The ideal candidate may be seen wearing a flag pin, holding children to show compassion, and looking rather stately. Through the power of our visual insight, we "pick up" when someone projects authority, control, power, and active leadership. We might even see this candidate interacting with famous people. Images of this person may include being seen at wealthy engagements or being photographed with a celebrity. They are often in the center of the photo. The goal for this candidate is to present an aura of status, be the center of attention, and show unspoken power. For example, a photo may be consumed by the "size" of the candidate and her eye contact staring down others in the photo. I want you to notice the image below that enhances the President's physical size, place in the center, and set mouth display to demonstrate his status.

President Donald Trump (C) walks with Senator Mitch McConnell, and Senator Roy Blunt as he arrives at a Senate Republican weekly policy luncheon at the US Capitol.

The populist candidate seeks to act "just like us." This candidate seeks mass appeal by being ordinary in large crowds. Large crowds in the background let the viewer know that this politician is one of them. He or she might also be viewed doing physical activities and exploring the outdoors. These photos may not place the candidate at the center of the shot. Cheering and clapping while waving placards with bold team names flood our views. Place the candidate within the crowd and a positive emotional connection hits us.

The populist candidate also wants us to know that he or she is ordinary and relates to our needs. Look at images of war heroes, firefighters, and public servants in uniform. Being seen with these national heroes confirms that candidates care about them. From veterans to senior citizens, handshakes and hugs demonstrate sincerity. You can't miss it.

Former Vice President Biden was slaughtered by the media for his inappropriate use of touch and space; images and videos show him embracing females or plopping a kiss on their heads. As well, President Trump's images of inappropriate space and touch consumption also make us take notice.

Barack Obama holds a young child during a campaign event at Bonanza High School on October 25, 2008.

Be aware of images and their deeper meaning. From holding children to smiling or displaying certain gestures, we, as viewers and voters, are either drawn in or become suspicious of a candidate's intention. Further, we subconsciously look for clothing colors that tend to be red, white, or blue to depict nationalism. Photos continuously imbedded with nationalism and patriotic loyalty scorch our brains. For example, look back at some of President Obama's photographs as he holds a small child with both back and front support. The viewer discerns that Obama is a caring person.

Humans judge physical formidability just by looking at photos of faces and bodies, according to the findings of one study. Our brains have mental representations for what a leader looks like and how he or she should operate in such leadership roles. Political candidates must understand that they cannot control every aspect of their political campaign, strategies, and media perceptions. Sometimes the feeling is too real, and sometimes the micro expression wasn't meant for public consumption.

Professionals alter images to create what Americans deem as ideal. Minor shifts of facial expressions can enhance a candidate's likability. A carefully placed hand on the shoulder denotes empathy, a strong handshake power and confidence, or perhaps the capturing of a tear confirms that this person cares.

Regardless of what feelings or thoughts are evoked from this image of US Representative Alexandria Ocasio-Cortez, I recommend that you suspend judgment of all photos until you understand all of the elements of a photo, image, or video.

It is also worth noting that, in photographs, the left side of the picture is considered the "power side." Why is this, you ask? It's simple: just by use of the hands. The person on the right of the photo must bend his or her wrist and arm at an odd angle to shake hands. This gives the person on the left the advantage. Additionally, the power person's left hand is able to easily wrap around the person on the right.

Even the term "incumbent" lends itself to being "in" by the very nature of the word. Now, "opponent" sounds eerily like opposition or opposite. And, who wants the opposite of being "in?" People, in general, will not risk something that they have in order to try something new. We do it at restaurants every day. We think we're going to try something new on the menu; yet, we play it safe with our favorite meal. The same holds true in the voting booth. Many think it's better to know what we have than to worry about what we might get.

Moving pictures, such as videos, produce stronger responses than photographs. Look at the influence of YouTube. In just a click, we are engaged with a clip, video, or monologue about a candidate. Relative to political information, television remains our primary source for information. In many homes, the TV even commands the most prominent position in the living room. Research confirms that television imagery does have an effect on how we vote and public opinion. News giants fight for our loyalty to their channel, their shows, and their agendas. We are easily persuaded.

Findings suggest that the inclusion of a visual element in a candidate's message will trigger a message in the viewer's mind as to what's important to that candidate. For example, watching a political candidate frequently engage with those who have health issues tell us voters that this politician will focus on the health of his or her constituents.

Campaign attacks, both verbal and visual, provide useful information during elections to better understand the media's slant, an interviewer's perception, or general expectations. Negative attacks are a part of political campaigns. Understanding the complexities of how they impact voter perceptions and guide decision making is important.

Men have higher status in American patriarchal society and roles. This should not transfer to work or public leadership roles. Higher status should not be defaulted to the masculine based on traditional tier structures. We must also fight our need to pigeonhole men. They have feelings which are overlooked at times. Think about how you feel about Democratic presidential candidate Mayor Pete Buttigieg—and his husband, Chasten Buttigieg. Does his sexual orientation evoke feelings from you? Do you associate his ability to lead our country based on your biases or perceptions? Really think about this.

Chasten Glezman Buttigieg greets his husband, South Bend, Indiana Mayor Pete Buttigieg, after he delivered a keynote address at the Human Rights Campaign's fourteenth annual Las Vegas Gala.

When we hear xenophobic, homophobic, or sexist remarks, or see someone displaying these negative attitudes or judgments, I suggest we directly address it. By staying quiet, this silence carries the communication of acceptance. People should, without retribution, challenge stereotypical views or prejudicial issues exhibited by their leaders or peers. Role segregation reinvigorates current stereotypical thinking and deters both men and women from going after leadership roles. I challenge you to start conversations about gender and social norms. Dismiss what the media feeds you and learn to feed yourself.

Physical appearance also influences how we select a candidate. We are drawn to specific features. Recount those from earlier chapters. Female candidates may need to use gender-neutral political platforms. When females "feminize" their campaigns, both males and females are negatively impacted according to a March 2018 study. For example, some question if Hillary Clinton should have used a gender-neutral slogan instead of her "I'm with Her" slogan. Fortunately, educated voters have more positive attitudes towards their party leaders of the same gender than those voters who are less educated. Voters with political interest and knowledge have more positive thoughts about their own party leader's gender.

Further, race is a factor, especially its use in TV ads. Who is with whom and in what context should race be studied? How is the ad staged? Sadly, race is a significant predictor of candidate support and most studies find that race is a factor impacting candidate preference by voters.

What do you see in this 2019 photo of Democratic presidential candidate Senator Cory Booker? A man? A black man? An angry man? A happy man? A presidential contender? I urge you to keep this single frame photo in context. Study the mixed message of this photograph and learn of its origin. Watch the entire video of his speech in South Carolina on June 22, 2019 and listen to his use of words like "Hope." "Opportunity." "Love." "God." "Uniting." Do those words align with his nonverbals? Watch the video for yourself. This Yale-educated candidate, like all candidates, should be judged based on a full assessment of background, platform, and experience.

However, this is no easy task. Actually, it's painstaking and time consuming. I recommend that you look for patterns in chosen pictures. Breakdown the photo into its elements, discerning what looks credible or staged. Images help us connect with candidates beyond text in that we are visual people and, as they say, "a picture is worth a thousand words."

By watching television, we are able to see candidates' verbal and nonverbal messaging. Moving (live) images are stronger than still photos. Yet, like photos, the angle of the camera, distance, and editing can and will influence our perceptions of candidates.

How the camera frames a candidate can taint that person's image by simply highlighting attributes or bashing elements about that person. This is also called second-level agenda-setting and we viewers fall into the trap frequently. While first-level agenda-setting gives power to the media for selecting issues and topics, this second tier of influence focuses on the power of the lens, framing attributes, and how an issue is defined for us.

The media sets the frame to focus on a candidate's dress, style, appearance, and other noticeable aspects of the person. Then, the media influences what they want us to see, hear, think, feel, and conclude. By manipulating attributes, perceptions vary from viewers and, many times, shifts to an emotional mindset rather than a thoughtful or cognitive frame of mind.

The way in which reporters select candidate action shots impacts how we voters think of these candidates. Media shots can make a candidate look positive by showing vigorously waving arms accompanied by a bright, gleaning smile. These supposedly happy shots draw us into an ad, an image, and a television clip. This, of course, works both ways. Regardless, the bulk of the power rests in the media's ability to pick and choose what clips they wish to spread across their various networks.

Personalized news stories, which include close-ups with testimonies, make us feel a part of their experiences. Being intentional about using a human face on social issues evokes strong emotions from us, the viewers. We seek to connect and comfort during sad or tragic stories.

A relative of a shooting victim kneels at a cross at a makeshift memorial site on June 2, 2019 in Virginia Beach, Virginia.

As social beings, we want to help people in pain. As a general rule when studied, personalized news stories run longer than their non-personalized versions. Add the political element and you can imagine the outcome. Take the above image from the 2019 Virginia Beach mass shooting and imagine how it became political bait.

When we watch emotional personalized stories, higher levels of political engagement are triggered, and we want to participate.

It is important to watch different media networks to learn their biases and how they portray political candidates. Do they focus on appearance, home lives, education, and the like? Do they equally compare each candidate running for office? Usually not. A review of camera angles, airtime, audio clips, still images, and anchor interview style and questions are tools in which voters are subject to buy in and, often, without even knowing about these biases.

Look at the image below. Focus on the picture and notice how it makes you feel. Actually, I propose you watch the entire two-part June 2019 Democratic debate on YouTube before you decide how you feel and think! Watch each candidate, listen to the issues, and focus on what is in front of you.

Kamala Harris and former Vice President Joe Biden speak as Sen. Bernie Sanders looks on during the second night of the first Democratic presidential debate on June 27, 2019 in Miami, Florida.

Social media, including Facebook and Instagram, are saturated with images. These images create a frame through which politicians seek to encourage voters to positively judge them. They want to be the ideal or the populist candidate. Some research suggests that a liberal-leaning media covers conservative scandals more than liberal scandals, and vice versa. This makes sense. It's much easier to point the finger at someone else rather than address one's own flaws and shortcomings.

Media experts focus on politician's nonverbals and draw conclusions for their audiences. For example, a BBC journalist called Mitt Romney "stiff and nervous" during a 2012 broadcast simply by looking at Romney's nonverbal behaviors. Interestingly though, it was not Romney's behaviors of nervousness that caught the journalist's eye, but rather Romney's lack of visible confidence. Negative visuals may draw voters' attention from their message due to the significant impact visuals have on people. While a candidate may be speaking her or his message, negative visuals, including questionable nonverbals or distractions in the image, weaken or shatter the candidate's message.

Front angle photographs are interpreted as honest in that you see it all and get what you see. Kress and van Leeuwen call this "an image act." The scene invites the viewer into the campaign as a participant. Cameras like to spotlight and exaggerate mistakes, mishaps, and slips of the tongue. One hand-to-face motion can draw hours of scrutiny from the media. The general rule of thumb is to under-act and be slow to react so that broadcasters don't jump on these nonverbals.

Advertising appeals during the political process. We may be motived to get involved, seek information, and be persuaded to pick a particular candidate. By clever uses of presenting enthusiastic candidates, situations, and behaviors, we are persuaded to act and make choices based on our emotions.

Digital media, blogs, and partisan news websites that cover the pros of one party, while questioning or bashing the ideas of the other, create emotional arousal in us. We identify with what we see and hear and become fiercely loyal and emotionally bound. Digital media is less costly and invites everyone to participate. Posted videos are free, and photographs, memes, clips, and blogs drench social media; however, the cost to news outlets is minimal. People do the work for free.

Online news sources are directly responsible for driving information into homes and eliciting behaviors from viewers. Many people are dependent on social media to gather information and learn about political candidates. From this, we are exposed to whatever spin the news wants to put on a story, as well as what emotions they want us to feel. As we gobble up information—often partisan—I warn you that we must be cautious.

Newspapers are also known for being biased or taking a conservative or liberal stance. It's common knowledge that the *Washington Post* is liberal, and *The Wall Street Journal*, owned by Fox, is conservative. In saying this, when a newspaper endorses a candidate, he or say may be shown in positive positions, including confident smiles and open-palmed hands or with the American flag waving in the background. Perhaps this candidate is photographed with a veteran or famous people in order to boost her or his image. On the other hand, when the media aims to attack an opponent, out comes the worst photos and clips, likely portraying the candidate as seedy, dark, and anxious.

One way to explore a dubious situation is through the questioning approach. Ask specific questions that force the other person to talk. Ask questions that go beyond yes and no answers. Encourage this person to talk about himself or herself and share details about the situation in question. You might be able to pick up on inconsistencies, shifts in tone and body, and cognitive loads, making it more difficult for the liar to keep his or her story straight. Again, ask for details. Most liars do not want to divulge more than they have to. Remember, these actors have practiced a lot and bank on standard lines of questioning and predictable questions—so unpredictable questions must be asked.

These information gathering opportunities provide a rich scenario from which we can examine the details. Use caution when you want to accuse and "think" the candidate is lying. Jumping to conclusions too early does not help your case, and confirms, again, that the liar is a pro. One interesting point that the research found was that liars may want to exclude details about other people in their fictious stories. Why? Because details may pique the curiosity of the other person and warrant further questions. Also, another person in the story may be questioned later and the liar is anxious about losing control of the storyline and details.

Be cautious as to not apply "liar" labels when we simply see eyes shift or lips being licked by the tongue. Liars may or may not look away. Many will stare and make "perfect" eye contact with you because they know the norms of eye contact in our society. As pointed out in Ekman's extensive work on lying and deceptive behaviors, we must use flexible decision rules, multiple cues, and time to catch a liar.

Evidence suggests that our attitudes and preconceptions influence how we process information, which also includes how we handle retractions. You can't just take it back. While we may acknowledge the "fact part" of the retraction, handling our feelings is not the same. The residue that remains from a situation may have an effect on our attitudes or may impact the climate or culture.

Along with becoming a nonverbal sage by cutting through the politics of political images, we cannot forget verbal words (though only seven percent of Mehrabian's rule) and how this form of communication is manipulated. Simon-Vandenbergen's extensive study of political narrative yielded some interesting and applicable information as we listen to candidates' words to secure our vote. The table below captures language and meanings for how politicians twist and imbed behaviors to keep us attached to them—regardless of issue or context.

Statement/Word	The Deeper Meaning
"It's my conclusion that . . . "	Emphasizes the validity of the claim. Candidate acts like an expert without citing sources.
"No one in their right mind . . ."	Defends the statement by inferring that only ignorant or crazy people would argue the claim.

"Crazy," "wild," and other negative behavior labels	Challenges the opponent's knowledge or reasoning. Provides a negative label for the challenger.
"If you were to . . ."	Acting like a teacher and voice of common-sense. Directing us as to what we should think or feel.
"Some . . ."	Plays down the claim. Does not trap the politician in an absolute. Certainty is weakened.
"Everybody . . ."	Making it appear that everyone should know the claim and we should as well.
"I heard that . . ."	Candidate personally validates the situation. Supposes a high degree of knowing something.
"I know ..."	Candidate has the knowledge. This knowledge may even act as the evidence. Appears to be truthful.
"I think that . . ."	Candidate's conclusion based on reason versus feeling.
"I'm happy that . . ." or "I'm glad to say . . ."	The candidate is satisfied about the claim. A feeling is attached to the candidate.

I highly recommend that you pay close attention to the manipulation of verbiage.

For example, when a candidate wants his/her words to appear factual, they may simply say the statement without referring to any source. The simplicity of this is clever, as we rarely ever challenge this method of demanding proof. Sometimes, to support the statement, they might even present it based on some story and then say, "This makes sense."

Statements like "I myself believe" and "I certainly think" express personal commitment to the claim without the need to verify with facts. "I" statements followed by "suppose" or "imagine" suggest that the candidate is not completely invested in the claim. Other personal involvement statements might include "I'm glad" or "I regret to say this." When a candidate acts regretful, we are drawn to his or her fallible human side. We may even forgive the person for the situation without quite knowing why. And, of course, we want the guilty party to look remorseful with sad eyes and a limp body. We might even expect a tear or two.

Kolenda's (2013) work on the methods of persuasion align with other researchers in that people come together when they are persuaded to do so. Understanding schema, priming, and spreading activation are important for political campaigns. How we communicate includes meaning making, sharing of information, and pulling others towards or away from someone or something.

So, what now? How will you vote? And, how will you know, definitively know, you picked the best person for the office?

I offer eye-opening suggestions to educate you with the hope of becoming a savvy, educated, and prepared voter.

Personally, and immediately:

- ☐ Raise your own awareness. Digest everything you just read for gender bias, indoctrinated stereotypes, fragile emotions, savvy liars, leaking body language, visual imagery, and round-the-clock media/social media.
- ☐ Be aware that television exposure of candidates' faces is a part of how you vote. How does TV or the media portray candidates? Favorably? Villainizing? Darker? Weary?
- ☐ Check your level of information for each candidate. What do you factually know? When you vote, you

have limited information, time, and energy for the entire political process. You will tend to default to what is the easiest in decision making and what is most homogenous to you. You will default to what you see and like.

☐ Understand the relationship between voting and facial features, TV airtime, political knowledge, and stereotypes associated with each, as you'll vote on these factors.

☐ Scrutinize your favorite media sources. Step back and observe news anchors' performances. Watch their facial expressions and body gestures. Listen to their word choices, as well. Do they use fear tactics? Do they tell you how to think and feel?

☐ Study the platform to glean information first. Is it an interview, debate, table conversation, or presentation on stage with a podium? These are initial clues as to how we expect a candidate to behave. It has been found that candidates will display more positive behaviors during interviews, but with formal and competitive settings like debates, anger and threat are seen more.

☐ Dissect ads and messages. Does the candidate opt to use stereotypes and fear tactics in ads or messages? Do you want someone who reverts to stereotyping as a way to burn an image into your voting brain?

☐ Consider your own biases and interpersonal skills with someone before you label them as deceptive. By paying attention to the wealth of nonverbals, hopefully you can figure out people's baseline behaviors, frequent word choices, and nonverbal cues.

☐ Having an open mind is very important when tuning into a candidate's speech (tone of voice) and body language. I know this can be exhausting, but you will learn a lot without being influenced by experts and journalists. We want to think that people are telling us the truth because we know that we'll be honest with them.

☐ Count candidates' nonverbals, including gestures, displays of emotion, and interactions with audiences for clues to evaluate them. Know their intentions. Do they match what they say?

☐ You might just pick your party affiliation. Whoever it is, you just check the Republican, Democrat, or Independent box. It won't be a surprise—you like your in-group. It's predictable.

☐ Watch their body language! You learned a lot from this book—apply it, please.

☐ Refer to the Worksheet after this chapter as a quick reference on your quest to know who the best choice is. Make copies and collect your data!

At your local governmental level:

☐ Invest in emerging leaders by providing them with networking opportunities and quality mentors. It takes a village, and younger generations will help with change.

☐ Make political arenas inclusive by volunteering to work various and politically different events. You will learn a lot.

☐ Hold organizations, including public service and government fields, accountable for reporting and mandate implementation plans. Policies on paper are just that: paper.

☐ Attend council meetings, work sessions, and events. Ask questions. Do your homework. Challenge the system.

☐ Acknowledge that society has an unequal balance of distribution of power between work, community, and home/family.

It is important to examine the core of our Commander in Chief's job description. I also think it's crucial to know who you vote into Congress. These representatives and senators provide the checks and balances required of our government and we vote them into office. By thoroughly analyzing the nuances of body language and nonverbal communication, you will be better prepared to select a leader who fits the real and complex interplay of task and social master.

Even though nonverbals are the biggest part of the formula for how you will rate candidates, the lasting impressions are significant on your feelings towards candidates. Back up your opinion!

Your own voting behaviors should not go unchecked. Recognize your own biases as you look, listen, and judge. The constant disregard of this plagues our country. You cannot objectively look at candidates, as your personal biases will always come into play in your decision making processes.

Your state of mind, or mood, will influence how you vote. If you are mad, most likely you'll act. I know, you feel how you feel, and you don't want to be forced to justify your feelings. They are yours. Just as your emotions of fear and empathy are strong, so are perceptions of prejudice. By the nature of the word, we all prejudge. Emotional recall is quick and strong. Emotional responses are quicker than rationale thoughts.

So, check your emotions. Check your facts. Then, check the box.

"One of the penalties for refusing to participate in politics is that you end up being governed by your inferiors."
—Plato

WORKSHEET
Politician Checklist

APPEARANCE: FIRST IMPRESSIONS OF THEIR OVERALL "LOOK"

- ☐ Clothes, colors, fit, and shoes.
- ☐ Hair style and color.
- ☐ Artifacts and accessories, pins, necklaces, rings, bracelets.
- ☐ Height in respect to others on stage.
- ☐ Standing or sitting.
- ☐ Position of hands and arms.
- ☐ Body size.
- ☐ Camera angles, the journalists, and the questions asked.

BODY PARTS

- ☐ Head, tilting, nodding, shaking.
- ☐ Eyes, contact, glasses, rolling, glaring, tired, blink rates.
- ☐ Mouth, smiling, showing teeth, biting lips, pursing lips, licking lips.
- ☐ Neck, rubbing or blanched.
- ☐ Hands, palms, fingers, thumbs, pointing, handshakes, or clapping.

☐ Arm positions, spread out or at side.

☐ Torso, shoulder shrugs, posture, slumping.

☐ Feet, stance and direction.

☐ Movements, pacing or rocking.

NON-SPEAKING: WHEN THEY ARE "LISTENING" TO ANOTHER PERSON. ARE THEY:

☐ Watching others.

☐ Taking notes and writing.

☐ Walking and pacing.

SOUNDS: TURN THE VOLUME ON

☐ Pitch, high, low, or changing.

☐ Speed.

☐ Pauses, number and length.

☐ Sounds like coughing or throating clearing.

☐ Accent.

☐ Use of words and vocabulary.

HOW THEY MAKE YOU "FEEL?" DO THEY LOOK?

☐ Aggressive

☐ Trustworthy

☐ Likeable

☐ Attractive

☐ Competent

References

Abusharha, A.A. (2017) Changes in blink rate and ocular symptoms during different reading tasks. Clinical Optometry 9 133-138. doi: 10.2147/OPTO.S142718

Ahler, D. J., Sood, G. (2018) The parties in our heads: misperceptions about party composition and their consequences. *The Journal of Politics, 80*, 964-981. doi: 104.171.248.009

Antonakis, J., Eubanks, D.L. (2017. Looking leadership in the face. Association for Psychological Science, 26(3), 270-275. doi: 10.1177/0963721417705888.

Asylum Channel (2011, January 11). Political Freudian Slips [Video file]. https://www.youtube.com/watch?v=Hpu_iEsISuI

Axtell, R.E. (1998) *Gestures: the Do's and taboos of Body Language Around the World,* New York, NY, John Wiley & Sons, Inc.

Bauer, N.M. (2017). Th effects of counterstereotypic gender strategies on candidate evaluations. *Political Psychology 38* (2), 279-295. doi: 10.1111/pops.12351

Banning, S., Coleman, R., (2009). Louder than words: a content analysis of presidential candidate's televised nonverbal communication. *Visual Communication Quarterly, 16* (1), 4-17. doi: 10.1080/15551390802620464

Barker, E. (2019, March 26). New neuroscience reveals 7 secrets that will make you persuasive. Retriever from https://www.bakadesuyo.com/2018/10/persuasive/

Bas, O., Grabe, M.E., (2016) Personalized news and participatory intent: how emotional displays of everyday citizens promote political involvement. *American Behavioral Scientist 60* (14), 1719-1736. doi: 10.1177/0002764216676247

Berggren, N., Jordahl, H., Poutvaara, P., (2010) The looks of a winner: beauty and electoral success, *Journal of Public Economics, 94*, 8-15. doi: 10.1016/j.jpubeco.2009.11.002

Bethel, S.M. (2009) *A New Breed of Leader: 8 Leadership Qualities that Matter Most in the Real World, What Works, What Doesn't, and Why*, New York, NY, Penguin Group (USA), Inc.

Blaker, N., Van Vugt, M. (2015) The status-site hypothesis: how clues of physical size and social status influence each other. *The Psychology of Social Status*, Chapter 6, 119-137. doi: 10.1007/978-1-4939-0867-7_6

Brader, T., (2005), Striking a response chord: how political ads motivate ad persuade voters by appealing to emotions. *American Journal of Political Science, 49* (2), 388-405

Brenan, M. (2017, November 16). Americans no Longer Prefer Male Boss to Female Boss. Retrieved from https://news.gallup.com/poll/222425/americans-no-longer-prefer-male-boss-female-boss.aspx

Bresnashan, J.Z., Zhu, Y., Anderson, J., Nelson, J. (2016) Obesity stigma and negative perceptions of political leadership competence. American Behavioral Scientist, 60(1) 1362-1377. doi: 10.1177/0002764216657383.

Bucy, E.P. (2016) The look of losing, then and now: Nixon, Obama, and nonverbal indicators of opportunity lost. *American Behavioral Scientist* 60(14) 1772-1798. doi: 10.1177/0002764216678279

Bucy, E.P., Dumitrescu, D. (2017) The body in politics- emotional, perceptual, and visceral dimensions. *Politics and the Life Sciences* 36(2) 1-2. doi: 10.1017/pls.2017.28

Bucy, E.P., Grabe, M.E. (2007) Taking television seriously: a sound and image bite analysis of presential campaign coverage, 1992-2004. *Journal of Communication* 57 652-675

Bucy, E.P., Stewart, P. (2018). The personalization of campaigns: nonverbal cues in presidential debates. Oxford Research Encyclopedia of Politics (on-line). doi: 10.1093/acrefore/9780190228637.013.52

Cassese, E.C., Holman, M.R., (2108) Party and gender stereotypes in campaign attacks. *Political Behavior*, 40:785-807. doi: 10.1017/s11109-017-9423-7

Cialdini, R.B. (1984, 1994, 2007) Influence: the Psychology of Persuasion, New York, NY, Harper Collins Publishers.

Chemi, E., Wells, N. (2019) Emotions, not facts, matter most in convincing voters. https://www.cnbc.com/2015/10/16/t-facts-matter-most-in-convincing-voters.html

Clifford, S. (2019) How emotional frames moralize and polarize political attitudes. *Political Psychology* 40(1) 75-91. doi: 10.1111/pops.12507

Coleman, R., Banning, S. (2006) Network TV news' affective framing of the presidential candidates: evidence for a second-level agenda-setting effect through visual framing. Journalism and Mass Communication Quarterly 83(2) 313-328

Conradt, S. (2015, June 15). Never Forget the Time Dan Quayle Misspelled "Potato." Retrieved from http://mentalfloss.com/article/64689/never-forget-time-dan-quayle-misspelled-potato

Diermeier, D., Li C. (2018) Partisan affect and elite polarization. *American Political Science Review* 113(1) 277-281. doi: 10.1017/S0003055418000655

Demir, M. (2011). Using nonverbal communication in politics. *Canadian Social Science, 7* (5). 1-14. doi: 10.3968/J.css.1923669720110705.199

Druckman, D., Bjork, R.A. (1991). *In the mind's eye: Enhancing human performance.* Washington DC: The National Academies Press.

Duerksen, K.N., Elias, L.J. (2018) Left wings to the left: posing and perceived political orientation. *Laterality: Asymmetrics of body, brain and cognition* 23(3) 364-376. doi: 10.1080/1357650X.2017.1362421

Dumitrescu, D., Gidengil, E., Stolle, D. (2015). Candidate confidence and electoral appeal: an experimental study of the effect of nonverbal confidence on voter evaluations. *Political Science Research and Methods 3* (1), 43-52. doi: 10.1017/psrm.2014.16

Dumitrescu, D. (2016). Nonverbal communication in politics: a review of research developments, 2005-2015. *American Behavioral Scientist 60* (14), 1656-1675.

Eagly, A.H., Heilman, M.E. (2016). Gender and leadership: introduction to the special issue. The Leadership Quarterly 27, 340-353

Ecker, U.K.H., Ang, L.C. (2019) Political attitudes and the processing of misinformation corrections. Political Psychology 40(2) 241-260. doi: 10.1111/pops.12494.

Ekman P. (2009) *Telling lies: clues to deceit in the marketplace, politics, and marriage.* New York, NY, W.W. Norton & Company

Ensari, N., Riggio, R.E., Christian, J., Carslaw, G. (2011). Who emerges as a leader? Meta-analysis of individual differences as predictors of leadership emergence. *Personality and Individual Differences 51*, 532-536. doi: 10.1016/j.paid.2011.05.017

Everitt, J., Best, L.A., Gaudet, D. (2016) Candidate gender, behavioral style, and willingness to vote: support for female candidates depends on conformity to gender norms. *American Behavioral Scientist* 60(14) 1737-1755. doi: 10.1177/0002764216676244

Frohne, U., Katti, C. (2000) Crossing boundaries in cyberspace? The politics if "body" and "language" after emergence if new media. Art Journal 59(4) 8-13. doi: 10.1080/00043249.2000.10792025

Fitzsimmons, T.W., Callan, V.J., Paulsen, N. (2014). Gender disparity in the C-suite: do male and female Eos differ in how they reach the top? *The Leadership Quarterly 25*, 245-266

Goman, C.K. (2018, August 26). *5 ways body language impacts leadership results*. Leadership Strategy. Retrieved from: https://www.forbes.com/sites/carolkinseygoman/2018/08/26/5-ways-body-language-impacts-leadership-results/#480b586f536a

Goodnow, T., (2013), Facing off: a comparative analysis of Obama and Romney Facebook timeline photographs. *American Behavioral Scientists.* *57*(11), 1584-1595. doi: 10.1177/0002764213489013

Gong, Z.H., Bucy, E.P. (2016) When style obscures substance: visual attention to display appropriateness in the 2012 presential debates. *Communication Monographs* 83(3) 349-372. doi: 10.1080/03637751.2015.1119868

Griffith, T. (1984, February 6) *Body-language politics.* TIME Magazine 123(6)

Hasell, A., Weeks, B.E. (2016) Partisan provocation: the role of partisan news use and emotional responses in political information sharing in social media. Human Communication Research 42 641-661

Hermann, M., Shikano, S., (2016), Attractiveness and Facial Competence Bias Face-Based Inferences of Candidate Ideology. *Political Psychology, 37*(3), 401-417

Hillary Clinton: Trump was a creep during our debates. (2017, August 23). *BBC.com.* Retrieved from https://www.bbc.com/news/world-us-canada-41023053

Ho, G.C., Shih, M., Walters, D.J. (2012). Labels and leaders: the influence of framing on leadership emergence. *The Leadership Quarterly, 23*, 943-952. doi: 10.1016/j.leaqua.2012.06.003

Hoyt, C.L., Murphy, S.E. (2016). Managing to clear the air: stereotype threat, women, and leadership. *The Leadership Quarterly 27*, 387-399

Hoyt, C.L., Simon, S., Reid, L. (2009). Choosing the best (wo) man for the job: the effects of mortality salience, sex, and gender stereotypes on leader evaluations. *The Leadership Quarterly 20*, 233-246. doi: 10.1016/j.leaqua.2009.01.016

Kaufmann, M.C., Krings, F., Zebrowitz, L.A., Sczesny, S (2017) Age bias in selection decisions: the role of facial appearance and fitness impressions. Frontiers in Psychology 8 1-14. doi: 10.3389/fpsyg.2017.02065

Kerevel, Y.P., Atkeson, L.R. (2015). Reducing stereotypes of female political leaders in Mexico. *Political Research Quarterly 68*(4), 732-744. doi: 10.1177/1065912915607637.

Kim, C. (2019) A white woman from Ohio asked Gillibrand about white privilege. Her answer was spot on. "What the conversation is about is when a community has been left behind for generations because of the color of their skin." *https://www. vox.com/policy-and-politics/2019/7/12/20691717/white-working-class-kirsten-gillibrand-white-privilege-institutional-racism*

Klofstad, C.A., Anderson, R.C. (2012), Sounds like a winner: voice pitch influences perception of leadership capacity in both men and women. *Proceedings of The Royal Society B. 279*, 2698-2704. doi: 10.1098/rspb.2012.0311

Klofstad, C.A. (2016). Candidate voice pitch influences election outcomes. *Political Psychology 17* (5), 725-738. doi: 10.1111/pops.12280

Kolenda, N. (2013). *Methods of Persuasion: how to use psychology to influence human behavior.* San Bernardino, CA. Kolenda Entertainment, LLC.

Kosiara-Pedersen, K., Hansen, K.M. (2014). Gender differences in assessments if party leaders. *Scandinavian Political Studies 38* (1), 26-48. doi: 10.1111/1467-9477.12033

Kraut, R.E. (1978). Verbal and nonverbal cues in the perception of lying. *Journal of Personality and Social Psychology, 36* (4), 380-391

Lang, C. (2019, February 6). Here's Why the Women of Congress Wore White for the 2019 State of the Union Address. Retrieved from https://time.com/5518859/state-of-the-union-2019-white

Lang, C. (2019, February 6). How Women in Congress Are Using Fashion to Send a Message. Retrieved from https://time.com/5520372/2019-state-of-the-union-fashion

Latner, M.S. (2019) Emotion, politics, and cooperation. *Politics and the Life Sciences 32*(2) 126-129

Lemoine, G.J., Aggarwal, I., Steed, L.B. (2016). When women emerge as leaders: effects of extraversion and gender composition in groups. *The Leadership Quarterly 27*, 470-486

Lepsinger, R. (2018, October 29). *How the best leaders master nonverbal communication.* Retrieved from https://www.business2community.com/leadership/how-the-best-leaders-master-nonverbal-communication-02133271

Lodge, M., Taber, C.S. (2005) The automaticity of affect for political leaders, groups, and issues: an experimental test of the hot cognitive hypothesis. *Political Psychology* 26(3) 455-485

Lippa, R.A. (2005). Beyond politics: a candid evaluation of gender differences. *Gender, Nature and Nurture (2nd ed.),* 105-107

Liu, S.S. (2019). Cracking gender stereotypes? Challenges women political leaders face. *Political Insight*

Lobinger, K., Brantner, C., (2015) Likable, funny or ridiculous? A Q-sort study on audience perceptions of visual portrayals of politicians. *Visual Communication*: 14(1): 15-40. doi: 10.1177/14703572114554888

Lukaszewski, A. W., Simmons, Z. L., Anderson, C., & Roney, J. R. (2016). The role of physical formidability in human social status allocation. *Journal of Personality and Social Psychology, 110*(3), 385. Retrieved from http://ezproxy.liberty.edu/login?url=https://search-proquest-com.ezproxy.liberty.edu/docview/1774915639?accountid=12085

Marcus, G.E. (2000) Emotions in politics. *Annual Review of Political Science* 3: 221-250

Masahiko, A. Patterson, D.P., (2019) Smiles, turnout, candidates, and the winning of district seats. *Politics and the Life Sciences,* 37(10): 16-31. doi: 10.1017/pls.2017.12

Mavin, S., Bryans, P., Cunningham, R. (2010). Fed-up with Blair's babes, Gordon's gals, Cameron's cuties, Nick's nymphets: challenging gendered media representations of women political leaders. *Gender in Management* 25 (7), 550-569. doi: 10.1108/17542411011081365

McGraw, K.M., (1998). Manipulating public opinion with moral justification. *The annals of the American academy of political and social science. 560*, 129+

McIlwain, C.D., Caliendo, S.M. (2009). Black Messages, White Messages. The differential use of racial appeals by black and white candidates. *Journal of Black Studies, 30* (5), 732-743. doi: 10.1177/0021934707299644

Mendoza, S.A., DiMaria, M.G. (2018). Not "with her": how gendered political slogans affect conservative women's perceptions of female leaders. *Published on-line.* doi: 10.1007/s11199-018-0910-z

Navarro, J. (2012, September 18). *10 effective ways leaders can influence others through nonverbal communications.* Retrieved from https://www.theartof.com/articles/10-effective-ways-leaders-can-influence-others-through-nonverbal-communications

Novotny, E., Carr, Z., Frank, M.G., Dietrich, S.B., Shaddock, T., Cardwell, M., Decker, A. (2018). How people really suspect and discover lies. *Journal of Nonverbal Behaviors 42*, 41-52. doi: 10.1007/s10919-017-0263-2

Okimoto, T.G., Brescoll, V.L. (2010) The price of power: power seeking and backlash against female politicians. *Personality and Social Psychology Bulletin 36*(7) 923-936. doi: 10.1177/0146167210371949

Olivola, C.Y., Sussman, A.B., Tsetsos, K., Kang, O.E., Todorov, A. (2012). Republicans prefer republican-looking leaders: political facial stereotypes predict candidate electoral success among right-leaning voters. *Social Psychological and Personality Science 3* (5), 605-613. doi: 10.1177/1948550611432770

Pelham, L., (2012, October 15). *Body language and politicians.* Retrieved from http://www.bodylanguageexpert.co.uk/body-language-politicians.html

Pinkney, V., Wickens, R., Bamford, S., Baldwin, D.S. Garner, M. (2014) Defensive eye-blink startle responses in a human experimental model of anxiety. Journal of Psychopharmacology 28(9) 874-880. doi: 10.1177/0269881114532858

Powell, G.N. (2011). The gender and leadership wars. *Science Direct 40*, 1-9. doi: 10.1016/j.orgdyn.2010.10.009

Researchers develop new software to detect lies. (2015, December 14). News Tonight. Retrieved from http://link.galegroup.com.ezproxy.liberty.edu/apps/doc/A437444191/STND?u=vic_liberty&sid=STND&xid=41255649

Rosette, A.S., Koval, C.Z., Ma, A., Livingston, R. (2016). Race matters for women leaders: intersectional effects on agentic deficiencies and penalties. *The Leadership Quarterly 27*, 429-445

Saint-Michel, S.E. (2018). Leader gender stereotypes and transformational leadership: does leader sex make the difference? *Dans Management* 21, 944-966

Sanbonmatsu, K., Dolan, K. (2009). Do gender stereotypes transcend party? *Political Research Quarterly 62* (3), 485-494. doi: 10.1177/1065912908322416

Schiller, D., Freeman, J.B., Mitchell, J.P., Uleman, J.S., Phelps, E.A. (2009). A neural mechanism of first impressions, *Nature Neuroscience* 12.4, 508+

Schneider, M.C., Bos, A.L. (2014). Measuring stereotypes of female politicians. *International Society of Political Psychology 35* (2), 245-266

Serazio, M. (2017) Branding politics: emotion, authenticity, and the marketing culture of American political communication. *Journal of Consumer Culture* 17(2) 225-241. doi: 10.1177/1469540515586868

Simon-Vandenbergen, A. (1996) Image building through modality: the case of political interviews. *Discourse & Society* 7(3) 389-415

Solomon, E.D., Hackathorn, J.M., Crtittendon, D. (2019). Judging scandal: standards or bias in politics. *The Journal of Social Psychology*, 159:1, 61-74. doi: 10.1080/00224545.2018.1453468

Steiger, R.L., Reyna, C., Wetherell, G., Iverson, G. (2019) Contempt of congress: do liberals and conservations harbor equivalent negative emotional biases towards ideologically congruent vs. incongruent politicians at the level of individual emotions? *Journal of Social and Political Psychology* 7(1) 100-1223

Talley, L., Temple, S. (2015). How leaders influence followers through the use of nonverbal communication. *Leadership & Organizational Development Journal 36* (1), 69-80

Thomas, N.A., Loetscher, T., Clode, D., Nicholls, M.E.R. (2012) Right-wing politicians prefer the emotional left. *PLoS ONE* 7(5) e36552. doi:10.1371/journal.pone.003655.

Tzu, Sun (circa 400 B.C.) *The Art of War*, translated by Yuan Shibing. New York, NY, Sterling Publishing Co., Inc

Vinkenburg, C.J., van Engen, M.I., Eagly, A.H., Johannesen-Schmidt, M.C. (2011). An exploration of stereotypical beliefs about leadership styles: is transformational leadership a route to women's promotion? *The Leadership Quarterly 22*, 10-21. doi: 10.1016/j.leaqua.2010.12.003

Vrij, A., Granhag, P.A., Porter, S. (2010) Pitfalls and opportunities in nonverbal and verbal lie detection. *Psychological Science in the Public Interest* 11(3), 89-121

Weisberg, H.F., Christenson, D.P. (2007). Changing horses in wartime? The 2004 presential election. Political Behavior 29, 279-304. doi: 10.1007/s11109-007-9026-9

Zhang, K., Franklin, L.A. (2013). Deception in context: coding nonverbal cues, situational variables and risk of detection. *Journal of Police Criminal Psychology, 28*, 150-161. doi: 10.1007/s11896-013-9127-9

Acknowledgments

Who would have thought starting out as a middle school teacher thirty years ago would have led me to this point. There is nothing as satisfying as taking my fascination with how teenagers think, feel, and behave and turning it into a career in communication and people processes. My curiosity for what makes us tick is never quenched. With the unwavering love of my parents, the joy of raising three children, and the loyalty of dear friends, my thirst for learning and relationships have taught me countless lessons. I am fortunate.

We don't get where we are without the help and guidance of those who care about us, and I have several who have forged the way for me. My greatest academic hero and mentor goes to my late friend, Dr. Roy Forbes, one of the kindest people I have ever known. His gentle words of encouragement helped me through my dissertation and I'll never forget him telling me that "great things are coming your way . . . you just don't know it." Truer words have never been spoken. I only wish that he could be here to celebrate with me. Perhaps he's with my Pop dancing among the stars.

For my parents, Grumpy and Frances Van Natten. These two taught me that I could do anything and told me I was the best kid ever. Don't you just love parents! I had role models who showed me love and resiliency so I could soar. And, watching my mom fight back from a stroke has only strengthened my belief that she is one strong lady and I admire her beyond words.

Evan Stichler, Jarrett Stichler, and Jillian Van Natten. Those are the sweetest names to type. I will always love you, spoil you, and support your dreams. You fill my world with joy, pride, and laughter; I wish for nothing more. Evan's Jenny and Jarrett's Courtney are two phenomenal young women who make my sons better with their love and I adore them both. Thank you. And, Courtney, thank you for introducing me to OneNote. You literally changed the writing game for me, and I thank you.

To my fiancé, Jerry Sterling. Talk about love! Your strength and unwavering belief in me still bewilders me. My soul loves your soul and our body language always talks. You edit my words, you listen to my speeches, you feed me and support me, and you drive me around. We have a grand life.

My gratitude goes out to my dearest friend and partner in crime, Shea Lox, educator, advocate, and lover of life. You are my 3 a.m. call and I appreciate those talks off the ledge, countless book edits, perspective chitchats, and bouts of laughter at the craziest of stories.

Thank you to my editor, Veronica (Ronnie) Alvarado and Skyhorse Publishing for piecing this puzzle together and answering my countless emails and questions. Ronnie, and the Skyhorse team, I am fortunate for your guidance throughout the process.

To Joe Narvarro who not only agreed to write the foreword for this book, but for being one of those guys who helps without anything in return. His encouragement and kind words were always what I needed to hear. I remain honored and humbled that he contributed to this book because he's one of the best at body language (I'm in opinion, the best).

To those certain people who were instrumental in making this happen, your knowledge, time, and thoughts make me a better person and I love being a part of your lives. Many are cited in these pages, and many more are not—but I know who you are.

Life is so much better going through it with all of these people. And, although there are many experts and researchers who contributed to this, any mistakes that are in this book are only mine.